RUSSIA

Uzlyan

OTHER BOOKS ON RUSSIA BY ROBERT G. KAISER
Cold Winter, Cold War
Russia: The People and the Power

Sichov

E. P. DUTTON || NEW YORK

RUSSIA FROM THE INSIDE

Text by Robert G. Kaiser ‖ Compiled & edited by Hannah Jopling Kaiser

Copyright © 1980 text by Robert G. Kaiser ‖ All rights reserved. Printed in the U.S.A. ‖ No part of this publication may be reproduced or transmitted in any form or by any means, electronic or mechanical, including photocopy, recording or any information storage and retrieval system now known or to be invented, without permission in writing from the publisher, except by a reviewer who wishes to quote brief passages in connection with a review written for inclusion in a magazine, newspaper or broadcast ‖ For information contact: E.P. Dutton, 2 Park Avenue, New York, N.Y. 10016 ‖ Library of Congress Cataloging in Publication Data ‖ Russia from the inside ‖ 1. Russia. I. Kaiser, Robert G., II. Kaiser, Hannah Jopling ‖ DK17.R868 1980 947 79-27303 ‖ ISBN: 0-525-14886-8 (cloth) ‖ ISBN: 0-525-47632-6 (paper) ‖ Published simultaneously in Canada by Clarke, Irwin & Company Limited, Toronto and Vancouver ‖ Designed by The Etheredges ‖ 10 9 8 7 6 5 4 3 2 1 ‖ First Edition

For Emily Eli Kaiser

The people who contributed the most to this book are the photographers whose work appears in it. We spent many hours in the new American homes of these former Soviet citizens, poring over their pictures, often drinking tea and conducting a good Russian conversation at the same time. We were shown enough good photographs to make half a dozen big books, and had to make many painful and arbitrary selections.

Helen Yakobsen, Olga Osmerkin and Leonid Lubinitsky all gave us invaluable help in tracking down photographers. Patty Forner was also generous with her time and assistance. Yuri Neymann and Nina Alovert kindly shared their photo collections with us.

Our work on this book often brought us to New York, where Herman and Suki Sandler, Alex Garvin, and Lee and Becky Lescaze repeatedly provided refuge and hospitality; we also had peace of mind knowing that Gladys Martin was looking after our children.

Most of the laboratory work for this book was done by Ed Burrows, whose attention to detail was invaluable. Ed had no previous experience in Russia or with Russian photographic equipment, and his reaction to the latter was revealing. How magnificent these pictures were, he said repeatedly, given the low quality of both Soviet film and the lenses these photographers often had to use.

Nancy Etheredge took the raw material of this volume and transformed it into a real album of elegance and style. We are especially grateful to her.

INTRODUCTION

This is a unique book, not because of its subject, but because of its contributors. Foreigners have been taking and publishing photographs of Russia for many years, and the Soviet government has sponsored photo albums of its own, but there has never been an uncensored collection of photographs of the ordinary scenes of Soviet life taken primarily by Soviet photographers. Many of the pictures in this book could have been taken by nobody else, because they reveal scenes that foreigners are not permitted to see.

Most of the photographers whose work is collected in this volume emigrated from the Soviet Union during the 1970s. None of them was able to bring out his entire collection of photographs, and many could bring only a few, but what they did preserve represents a fascinating glimpse of Russia from the inside.

Foreigners have long belabored the mysteriousness of Russia. There are enigmatic aspects of Russian life, but they have been exaggerated. Much of what outsiders have found mysterious is simply a little *different*. Or so we will argue here.

There is a theory behind this book: that a human society, no matter how complex or baffling to outsiders, creates reliable and visible evidence about its own true nature. To put the theory argumentatively, a human society is like an elephant: Neither can be understood at a glance, but the outward characteristics of both, carefully studied, provide extremely revealing clues about the entire organism.

But if Russia consists largely in what meets the eye, an important question remains: Whose eye? Few outsiders get the chance to let their eyes roam freely inside the Soviet Union. More than half the country is simply closed to foreigners, *zakrit*, as the Russians say, often with grand finality, as though that was that. What is open is not entirely open, since Russians discourage outsiders from seeing any of their dirty linen, or indeed anything that they consider embarrassing.

The first Russian city we visited was Khabarovsk, an industrial center at the far eastern edge of Siberia, near Japan. Khabarovsk was settled in the last century by Russian pioneers who built handsome versions of the traditional Russian log house, and many of them were still in use when we visited. When I showed an interest in photographing these houses, our Intourist guide gave me a stern lecture. Why did I care about those old houses? They would soon be torn down anyway. Why didn't I take pictures of the new, modern Khabarovsk?

Hull

Suzdal.

And that was a superficial embarrassment. Had we asked to see the city prison, for example, or one of the bunkhouses for drunks that are a typical feature of Soviet life, the answer would surely have been *nyet*. Intourist guides are programmed for museums, war memorials, cultural events, and the occasional showpiece factory, but not for tours of real life in the USSR. Real life is not supposed to be any outsider's business.

Potemkin villages were invented in Russia, and this was probably no coincidence. (The name comes from Prince Potemkin, an official in the reign of Catherine the Great, who had constructed false-front "villages" along the Volga. When the empress sailed down the river she got the impression that vacant areas were actually inhabited.) Today it is a basic part of Soviet life to do things simply for show, or so one can boast of having done them. This is so common that the Russians have invented a slang word to describe it—*pokazukha*, based on the verb that means to show or show off.

On that same visit to Khabarovsk—our first exposure to the standard Soviet treatment for foreign visitors—a journalist who was our principal host took us to a factory that manufactured wire cable. We had a rare opportunity, he said, to see a factory seldom visited by foreigners, a statement I took at face value until later, when the official showing us around the factory broke off our conversation to make a phone call. Perhaps not realizing that we spoke Russian, the factory official explained to the person he called that he was temporarily tied up "in the Intourist room." In other words, foreign tourists were brought to this factory so often that a room had been set aside for the purpose. So much for our host's assurances.

In the years that followed we were the victims of *pokazukha* again and again, but eventually we at least learned to recognize it. We came to expect to be shown only the best factories, the glossiest collective farms or the most benign museums. Russians take this so thoroughly for granted that they expect foreigners always to do the same thing. A member of the politburo on a tour of Canada several years ago chastised his hosts for trying to fool him by filling the parking lot of a factory he was taken to visit with cars, as if to suggest that ordinary workers drove their own automobiles to work. You didn't have to go to such lengths to try to impress me, the Russian told his hosts.

Only a man who was familiar with elaborate efforts to impress foreigners could have made such a remark. In fact, members of the politburo are extremely familiar with such tactics, and employ them all the time. We now know, for instance, that the Soviet space program in the 1950s and early 1960s was a scientific Potemkin village itself, a razzle-dazzle effort to "beat the Americans" based on expediency and technological bravura, but lacking in the basic ingredients that would have allowed the Soviets to compete seriously in the race to the moon, say. In fact, there was no race to the moon; the Russians were never in a position to enter such a race. But their ingenious ability to make a crude initial space program look formidable set the United States off on an arduous and expensive chase.

Showing off appeals to Russians. This is part of Russian ambivalence toward foreigners, and also part of Russia's historic ambition to be taken seriously in the world, to be a great power. A mixture of isolation and exposure, competition and humiliation, disaster and triumph has typified the Russian experience with the outside world, particularly the West. Russians are terrified of foreigners, sometimes all but paralyzed with feelings of inferiority, sometimes emboldened by anxiety to overreach or overstate their case. Foreigners are intrigued with Russia, wary of Russia, and constantly looking for Russia, trying to discover what really is there.

Russia From the Inside is not the typical picture album of beautiful photographs and pretty scenes, but an attempt to challenge stereotypes and go behind closed doors to reveal as much as possible about the Soviet Union today. The photographers whose work appears here did not depend on Intourist guides to show them around. Most of them are Russians themselves, Russians who emigrated from the Soviet Union during the last few years and now live in the West. With the eyes and instincts of natives, these photographers took pictures of scenes that tourists never see—not just the trunk of the elephant, but the whole pachyderm, even inside the deep creases of the skin.

Their photographs reveal the basic facts—the basic contradictions, as a good Marxist might put it— of the Soviet Union today. They show a big, rough, muscular, sometime beautiful country filled with a rich variety of humankind. They show the fruits of a crash program of modernization that has pushed the Soviet Union pell-mell into the industrial age while leaving parts of the country all but untouched. They show the formality and pomposity of Soviet official functions, where form and ap- pearance are always more important than substance.

And, most important, they reveal the Russians as people. We come to know the tightly knit Russian family so devoted to children, the Russian enthusiasm for nature and her works, the daily business of keeping a home and working at a job, the loneliness of growing old, and the rituals of death.

All of this is visible to the eye. There are certainly secrets in the Soviet Union—secret meetings of the politburo, secret doings of the political police (the KGB), secret installations for the manufacture of weapons—but the secrets do not contradict the visible evidence. Put another way, what you see in this book is true, revealing, and significant evidence about a society that need not seem as mysterious as it does.

Valuable as it is, however, visible evidence cannot explain a society's traditions nor its history; noth- ing that meets the eye reveals the Russian sense of humor or the contemporary Russian attitude (at home, not in public) toward Marxism-Leninism. Therefore, words are also necessary to clarify what the camera cannot capture.

Russia is an isolated country, geographically and historically. Czars and commissars have collaborated to surround old Russia with docile neighbors. Russians have had extended expo- sure to foreigners only when the foreigners came uninvited: the Mongols in the Middle Ages, the French in the nineteenth century, the Germans in the twentieth century. On the whole, Russians

Antsis

Hull

Kiev.

Near Suzdal.

The Ukraine.

have lived alone, perched above Europe in their own special corner of the globe, much nearer the Arctic than the equator.

The antecedents of the Russian state go back 1,100 years. This is a staid and ancient culture, always separate from Europe's, always particularly and peculiarly Russian. Perhaps because of its isolation and its uniqueness, Russia has always regarded foreigners and foreign influences with fear, sometimes tinged with awe or admiration.

Nearly all the great ideas and movements that shaped modern Europe, and thereby America, passed Russia by. The Russians chose the Eastern Orthodox Church, so missed the struggle between Catholicism and Protestantism. The intellectual and political ferment that produced the American and French Revolutions in the eighteenth century and gave the West its liberal tradition missed Russia entirely. The Industrial Revolution reached Russia only at the end of the nineteenth century, and then largely because foreigners imported it.

But if the Russians have always lived apart from Europe and the West, they have always maintained a connection, too. Peter the Great, the most resourceful of the czars, pointed Russia westward in the early eighteenth century when he decided to build a new capital on the Gulf of Finland, a "window on the West" and also a mirror of the West, designed largely by Italian and French architects. Petersburg became a European city, a seat of culture much admired in Europe, and a symbol of the possibility that Russia could become a real part of Europe. By the first years of this century it appeared that Russia was indeed joining Europe, casting off its primitive and Asian ways and speeding into the industrial age. But the Bolsheviks' seizure of power in 1917 changed Russia's course.

Communism was a European idea, and Lenin considered himself an internationalist, not just a Russian—an agent of the international proletariat, a herald of the future that was all Europe's destiny. But Europe failed to cooperate, and by the time of Lenin's premature death in 1924, his creation, the USSR, was alone and quite lost, no longer so close to Europe and unsure of where it was headed.

Joseph Stalin created a new future for Russia. Stalin abandoned Lenin's equivocal domestic policies, and insisted on imposing a genuine revolution from above on all of Russia and its empire. He "collectivized" the peasantry—in the 1920s the vast majority of the population—by wiping out the middle-class peasants and reorganizing the countryside into collective farms. He virtually dictated a great economic leap forward with the first of many Five-Year Plans, exacting enormous exertion from the growing urban population to give Russia a real industrial infrastructure.

Much of Stalin's original accomplishment was destroyed in World War II, what Russians call "the Great Patriotic War," when 20 million of them perished in a devastating but ultimately heroic venture. But the cardinal elements of Stalinism survived the war and survive to this day, with a few important exceptions.

Stalin transformed Russia into a giant, centralized bureaucratic structure, establishing "The Plan" as the guiding force in the nation's life. Year after year, industrial ministries and the State Planning Commission in Moscow set new, higher targets for factories and enterprises. They responded by replacing the losses suffered in the war, then pushing ahead to levels of wealth and production that eventually surpassed those of the traditional European powers.

Leningrad.

Poliakov

Leningrad.

Stalinist centralization went well beyond the economy. Few aspects of Soviet life escaped it. Cultural activities were organized into giant national "unions"—of artists, writers, composers, etc. The unions, run by political factotums, could dominate all of the arts. The army and supporting institutions became a central pillar of the state. The political police grew and prospered. The Communist party became a monster bureaucracy that cast a shadow in every corner of Soviet life, providing both cohesion and discipline to a society that needed both. When discipline failed, Stalin turned to terrorism. He terrorized every element of the population, including the highest ranks of the Party, army, and political police, to sustain his dictatorship and satisfy his own madness. He killed millions of people and terrified the rest, scaring off potential critics or opponents long before they dared open their mouths.

One of Stalin's principal objectives was to make the Soviet Union self-sufficient, to cut it off from the outside world to the maximum feasible extent. Eventually it became a capital offense for a Soviet citizen even to talk with a foreigner without authorization. By the time of Stalin's death in 1953 the country was all but totally isolated. The economy was organized to maximize self-sufficiency. As described in official propaganda, the world outside was filled with hostile forces determined to destroy the Soviet state.

Stalin's successors decided that they could not—or would not—maintain that isolation. In 1956 the first western tourists in many years were allowed to visit the USSR. Soviet leaders began to travel the world, to attend international conferences and eventually to enter into negotiations with other governments.

Exposure to the outside world became infectious. Throughout the 1960s and 1970s it grew, so that Russia is now much less isolated than it was just twenty-five years ago. But the Soviet experiment with relaxed East-West relations was not a great success. The decade of the 1970s was not long enough to purge the old instincts in East or West, as the invasion of Afghanistan and the subsequent collapse of "detente" revealed. As we completed this book early in 1980, the prospects for future cooperation between the Soviets and the western world were cloudy.

Even in the warmest days of East-West detente, the Russians never lost the old uneasiness about foreigners and foreign influences. Foreign tourists were allowed to come to the Soviet Union, but with rare exceptions Soviet citizens have not been allowed to travel to the West. The Soviet authorities are anxious to impress foreigners with their country's accomplishments, but not willing to let them roam freely or see things that might be embarrassing. Many of the scenes in this book still could not be seen by an ordinary foreign tourist.

The Russian attitude toward foreigners is one example of a gaping national inferiority complex that is a central element of life in the modern Soviet Union. Without some understanding of it, an outsider cannot hope to grasp what the country is really like.

The Kremlin, Moscow.

Insecurity starts at the very top. The men who rule the USSR were not elected to their positions of leadership. They do not enjoy the self-esteem that comes from birth into a royal family. They are the heirs of usurpers, the original Bolsheviks, and they have none of the legitimacy that elected or even inherited leadership status provides. In other words, the men in the politburo cannot be sure they deserve to be there.

That is why they react so harshly to the tiny band of dissidents who have appeared in recent years to challenge the arbitrary nature of Soviet power. The dissidents have no apparent political influence. Their desire for a freer, more liberal society is not widely shared by ordinary Soviet citizens. Yet the KGB pursues them as though they were dangerous enemies of the state. Dissident intellectuals convicted in Soviet courts for "disseminating anti-Soviet material" have received sentences of seven years at hard labor plus five years of "internal exile," or mandatory residence in a remote corner of the country. As small in number and powerless as they are, the dissidents apparently terrify the Soviet leadership, probably because they are a reminder that Soviet leaders are not guaranteed the allegiance of their people—that they could be challenged. Strong, secure leaders can endure criticism and opposition, but the Soviet politburo will indulge almost none.

Insecurity also explains the bluster and tension that typify Soviet negotiations with foreigners. Businessmen from the capitalist world find Moscow a hard place to do business, primarily because, as one man who has spent a lifetime trading with the Russians once put it, "every negotiation is based on suspicion, mistrust." This businessman had tried repeatedly to convince his Soviet partners that he and they could both benefit from the same deal, but they never seemed to believe him: "They're always implying that you're trying to trick them, fool them." The process is similar in political negotiations; among diplomats, the Russians have an unenviable reputation for nastiness and rigidity.

The Russian inferiority complex helps explain Soviet pretensions in world politics. For centuries Russians have dreamt of being taken seriously in world affairs, and at certain important moments they have been. But only in the last generation has the Soviet Union achieved the military strength and political influence to become a major power and a factor in every nation's calculations. The urge to be admired or feared is an old Russian attribute.

Insecurity also explains what is most baffling to many outsiders about Soviet life, the apparent docility of the masses. Even Poles and Hungarians wonder at the all-suffering patience of the Soviet people, and westerners can find it astounding. But the Soviet masses are a special category of humanity. They don't know much about life in Poland, Hungary, or—especially—the West, where the standard of living is much higher than in the USSR. They know only their own deprived past—slavery barely a century ago (Russia's serfs were freed in 1861), poverty, revolution, war, Stalin's terror, war again, more poverty and deprivation. In modern times the Soviet regime has brought stability, predictability, and a measure of prosperity to its citizens. It has provided security in the most basic sense: enough to eat, a reasonable place to live, no invasions and no wars. For a people so long denied these basic comforts, contemporary Soviet life is a pleasure, at least in relative terms. Instead of complaining, for example, that they live worse than the people of Yugoslavia, Russians tend to exult that they live so much better than their own grandparents or parents.

This thought leads to a second aspect of Russian life that must be grasped by anyone seeking to understand the Soviet Union now. That is the extraordinary continuity between old Russia and the modern Soviet Union, the preservation of Russian folk culture, and the survival of a basic Russian psychology or national character.

Moscow.

Norilsk.

Old customs of childrearing have been passed on for countless generations. Russians still swaddle their babies, wrapping them up tight for long periods in infancy, a deprivation of freedom which the famous child psychologist Erik Erikson has argued is a form of preverbal indoctrination that teaches Russians to feel they need to be rigidly restrained for their own good. Russian mothers learn and pass on old verities: Never let a baby sleep on its stomach; bathe a baby only in boiled water, and only if there is enough of it to submerge the child thoroughly; and many more.

An old Russian sense of the appropriate role of a national government has also survived into the Soviet era. The first Russian state in the eighth century, as well as the historians can determine, was established by a Scandinavian prince whom Russian tribes had invited into their land to rule over them and protect them from outsiders. The protection was what they needed most. Since then, Russians have accepted their state authority as a source of order and security to which various kinds of tribute must be paid. The western idea of a government that exercises sovereignty conferred on it by the people, and is thus answerable to the people, makes no sense to an ordinary Russian. That is literally a foreign idea.

In many ways the Bolsheviks perpetrated a superficial revolution, simply finding new forms for old Russian arrangements. This was especially true of Stalin's dictatorship, which echoed czarist Russia to an uncanny degree, though it was harsher. Stalin reinstituted an elaborate hierarchy of rank, substituted Marxist-Leninist orthodoxy for Orthodox Christianity (though it too survived), and reestablished the notion that life throughout the Russian Empire should revolve around a single autocratic personality. (Today the autocracy has become a collective affair.)

"The fundamental and most stable feature of Russian history," wrote Leon Trotsky in the famous opening line of his *History of the Russian Revolution,* "is the slow tempo of her development, with the economic backwardness, primitiveness of social forms and low level of culture resulting from it." Though much of the period since the Revolution in 1917 has been devoted to contradicting Trotsky's assertion, it remains essentially accurate. Russia's persistent poverty, backwardness, and inefficiency are the third important aspect of Russian life that an outsider needs to appreciate to understand the contemporary Soviet Union.

This is not an easy point for many in the West to grasp or accept. We have been buffeted by windy propaganda, both from the USSR and from our own government, about the power of the Soviet state. Early Soviet successes in space, Soviet ability to all but match American weaponry, and the general perception that the United States and the Soviet Union are two essentially comparable "superpowers" have—with other factors—lulled much of the outside world into a profound misunderstanding of the true nature of the Soviet system.

Here, happily, pictures *do* help explain the truth probably better than words. Pictures can reveal the surprising sloppiness of Soviet workmanship, the primitive level of Soviet agriculture, the poverty in which many Soviet citizens live. If they are honest, though, pictures will also show impressive new Soviet factories, advanced scientific laboratories, and other symbols of genuine Soviet achievements. Yet, pictures cannot easily explain away the apparent contradiction between these two extremes.

In fact, there is no real contradiction between Soviet backwardness and Soviet accomplishments. The two coexist because the resources expended for the accomplishments ensure the backwardness of much else. What may be hardest for westerners to grasp is the way a centrally planned economy works. In the Soviet Union resources are only used for purposes that central political authorities have approved. If those authorities want a society that manufactures neither dog food nor dishwashers, they can will it so—as indeed the Soviet leaders have. If they wish to spend disproportionate sums on the manufacture of missiles or the training of ballet dancers, they can do that too—as they have.

The Steppe.

Grigorovitch

Kaiser Sochurek

Dagestan.

Siberia.

Uzbekistan.

But success in a limited number of areas should not be able to conceal the Soviet Union's many economic, managerial, and technological failings. It is no coincidence that the Russians have been spending billions of dollars to buy machinery, and even entire factories, from the capitalist world. But these purchases can do little to solve the country's underlying economic problems, though they do help fill specific gaps in the Soviet economy.

The USSR is a poor nation. Fresh meat is a costly rarity in much of the country, all but unheard of in many places. Soviet citizens live in crowded, inadequate housing; more than a third of them must share living space in some kind of communal quarters. Most households have no telephone and few, if any, modern appliances. Clothing is expensive (a month's salary for a man's suit, for example) and often shoddy. Old Russia has been transformed—electrified, industrialized, modernized, built and rebuilt—yet compared to the capitalist world, Trotsky's description still applies.

But despite all these failings, Russia holds a power over her own people as ferocious as any patriotism known to man. An outsider must also understand this power to get any sense of the real Russia. Nikolai Gogol described it in his nineteenth-century masterpiece, *Dead Souls:*

> Everything in you is poor, straggling and uncomfortable: no bold wonders of nature crowned with ever bolder wonders of art, no cities with many-windowed tall palaces built upon rocks, no picturesque trees . . . Everything in you is open, empty, flat; your lowly towns are stuck like dots upon your plains . . . There is nothing to beguile and ravish the eye. But what is the incomprehensible, mysterious force that draws me to you? Why does your mournful song, carried along your whole length and breadth from sea to sea, echo and re-echo incessantly in my ears? What is there in it? What is there in that song? What is it that calls, and sobs, and clutches at my heart? . . . Russia! What do you want of me? What is that mysterious, hidden bond between us?

This book is meant to create an impression, not exhaust the subject. We have chosen about 200 photographs, and hope that each one of them conveys something important about the contemporary Soviet Union. The photographs that accompany this introduction are meant to set the scene by evoking the appearance of the country. Later sections are devoted to specific aspects of Soviet life. Inevitably, many scenes that might have been included, had we found the right photographs, or had we decided on a longer book, are missing.

EVERYDAY LIFE

Literally translated, the Russian version of "How are you?" is "How are you living?" A typical answer these days is, "We're living well!"

Russians' enthusiasm for the way they live may baffle visitors from richer lands, by whose standards the Russians aren't living well at all. But Russians don't live by foreigners' standards; they live by their own. Russians instinctively tend to think that the real world ends at their own country's borders. The Soviet system that now controls their country reinforces their isolation. So Russians measure their lives by an inherited standard of comparison with their own past. And by that standard, they really are living well—much better than their parents, incomparably better than their grandparents.

The Soviet system has transformed Russian life. The ordinary folk whose forebears were peasant slaves until 1861, and whose country was devastated as recently as World War II, are today safe and secure. They are likely to be living in a Soviet city or town in a modest private apartment; they have access to free medical care, free schools, cheap public transport, television, and many of the other conveniences of modern civilization. This is how a majority of Russians now live.

Nevertheless, old traditions still govern much of human existence in Russia. From the birth of a new child to the death of an ancient *babushka,* Russians follow rituals and folk customs that are much older than the Bolshevik Revolution. A Russian may be proud of his modern apartment, but he would no more shake hands with a visitor across its threshold than his grandfather would have done so through the door of his peasant *izba* a century or more ago—bad luck.

For expectant mothers, peasant wisdom dictates long walks every day and no sweets (they make the skin itch). Birth itself—traditionally and in fact—is an ordeal to be survived, not a pleasure. Pregnant women receive only vague instructions on how to give birth: Oxygen helps, so breathe deeply, and rub your stomach with circular strokes to ease the pain of contractions. The more elaborate training now common in the West for women who want to give birth without an anesthetic is unknown in Russia (though the Lamaze method of natural childbirth is said to be based on Russian research). But Russian women in labor are not offered anesthetic except in emergencies. Typically, they give birth in large delivery rooms where one or two other women may be having their babies at the same time.

Tulchinsky

A Soviet delivery room.

Russians share a national phobia about germs. A new infant may be kept apart from its mother for twenty-four hours or more for fear of infection. Visitors are banned from maternity homes, and mothers are kept in them for ten days; so a new father must be patient waiting to meet his son or daughter—or to comfort his wife.

Fathers are usually banned from the maternity home for ten days after birth, on the theory that they might expose mother or child to dangerous germs. So the eventual reunion can become quite an event. These fathers are waiting to greet their wives and new children at the end of their ten-day wait.

When the baby finally arrives at home, the entire extended family throws itself into the raising of the new creature. The new arrival quickly becomes the center of the whole family's attention. The child retains this exalted status until he leaves the familial nest as a young adult.

Russians assume that children cannot and should not do much of anything for themselves; so they are indulged and protected for many years. This starts in infancy, when Russians still wrap their babies tight in swaddling clothes. Mother or grandmother feeds a child until it is five or six years old, and dresses it even longer. Children are not allowed to play outside by themselves until they are six or seven. Rules of behavior can be harsh; for example, if the child is playing in the sandbox, under no circumstances should its bottom touch the damp sand—unhealthy!

New arrivals in the nursery.

Outside a pediatric clinic in Moscow.

Check-up.

Outside a pediatric clinic in Siberia.

The rules and traditions are accepted by virtually all parents, a tribute to the homogeneity of Russian life. So in winter, all Russian children are wrapped up in similar fashion: thick wool coats, felt boots, snug hat, wrapped and stiffened by a long scarf. The outfit forces the children to waddle along like small penguins, but they are *warm!*

Russian parents seem universally to believe that hiccups are caused by drafts or an impending head cold. They accept the inherited wisdom that left-handedness is bad, so all children are compelled to be right-handed. This can begin in the sandbox, where mothers will insist that little Volodya only use his shovel with his right hand.

Like so many aspects of Soviet life, childrearing is a no-frills experience. The gadgets and appliances that have simplified parenthood in the rich capitalist countries have only just begun to reach the Soviet Union. Few Russians have their own washing machines, for example, and Soviet shops do not sell diapers. Old sheets or towels are recommended for that purpose. There are no waterproof rubber pants, no liquid vitamins or aspirin for children, and almost no commercial baby food.

Most mothers hold full-time jobs. They are entitled to a year off for a new baby, but after a year they lose their old positions if they don't return to work. This leaves much of the childrearing to *babushka*—if one of the grandmothers is available—or, increasingly, to state institutions that care for children from the age of three months. By age four, the majority of Soviet children are enrolled in state kindergartens, where they receive their first instruction in reading and writing (much easier to learn than English, thanks to the consistently phonetic and predictable Russian language) and also their first political lessons, mostly inspirational instruction on the life of Vladimir Ilyich Lenin.

Kindergarten introduces a Russian child to the Soviet system of education. In drawing class, for example, the kindergarten teacher will post a picture in the front of the room and ask each child to copy it. Personalized examples of self-expression are neither prized nor solicited. At school, which begins at age seven, the child finds a stern, almost Victorian atmosphere. The girls all wear pinafore uniforms, the boys gray suits. Every classroom is organized in rows of old-fashioned wooden desks. The teaching method is old-fashioned, too; students are expected to memorize and recite, memorize and recite. When they want to contribute in class, children are expected to raise their hands in a particular way. The teacher is looking for a single right answer, and a single right way of arriving at it. Throughout his years in school and university, a Russian child will find no encouragement to do orig-

Kaiser

The state provides an increasing number of places in day-care centers for children from three months to three years old. These one-year-olds are in a nursery in Volgograd, where most of them spend ten hours a day. The apparatus in back of their playpen is to help them learn to walk.

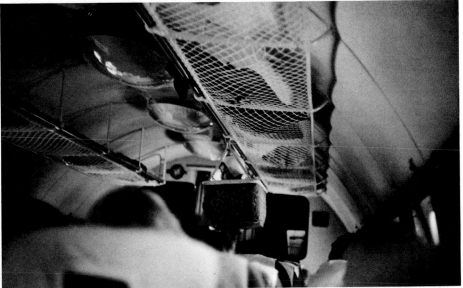

Stone

Precious cargo. An infant in its bassinet hangs from the baggage rack of a Soviet airliner.

Babushka knows best.

Uzlyan

Soviet kindergartens teach the
right way to write
(right-handed), the right way to
draw (duplicate the teacher's
drawing), even the right way to
sleep at naptime.

Kindergartners in Kiev dressed up for a New Year's party.

Antsis

Sochurek

Antsis

Recess in Siberia. The children are queueing neatly for a turn sliding down an icy slide.

First day of school. This is the only day of the year when the girls wear their white pinafores.

Walking to school

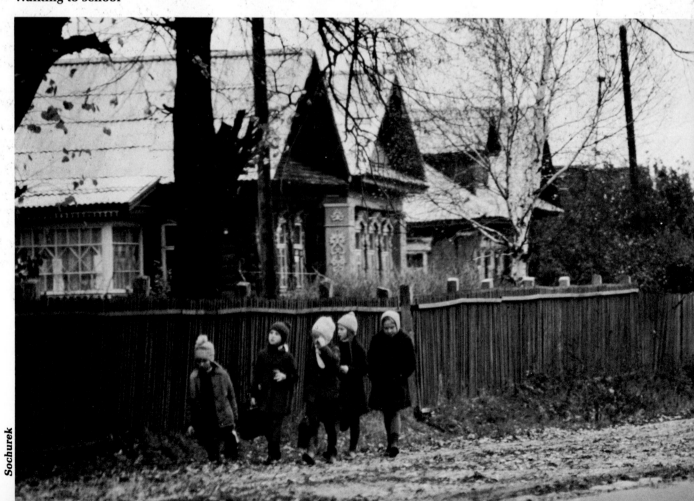

inal or creative work. Soviet educators show no interest in the idea that children ought to learn to think for themselves and come to their own conclusions.

None of this can overpower the traditional impulses of childhood, however. Russian kids are thoroughly kids—frantic and frenetic, unpredictable and sometimes uncontrollable. Teachers complain that they can't maintain the old-style discipline; kids revel in the discovery of their own power to frustrate the adult world.

Grandfather Frost, the Soviet version of Santa Claus, brings his gifts on New Year's eve.

Sandler

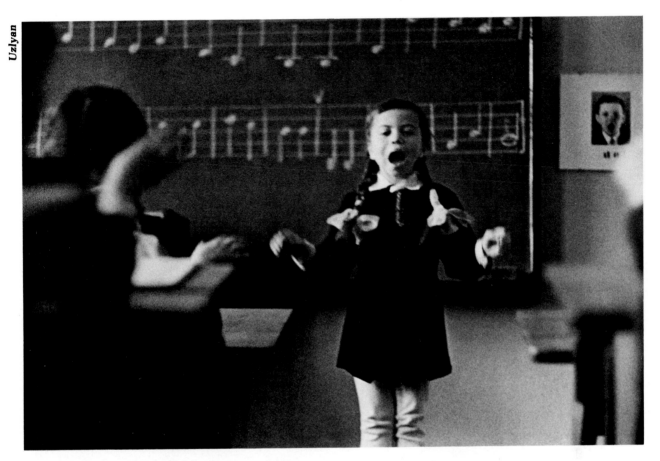

Uzlyan

A school of the arts for gifted children in Vilnius.

The dramatic improvement in Russian living conditions since World War II has created a younger generation whose childhood has had little in common with that of their own parents. This new generation knows nothing of the ravages of war, the terrorism of Stalin's dictatorship, or the physical hardships of the war and postwar years. There are all the makings of a generation gap here. The younger generations may well grow up with entirely new expectations for what life should be like.

Indeed, this has started to happen. Numerous Soviet teenagers have succumbed to the wiles of western, mostly American, pop culture. A pair of blue jeans is a prized possession, sold on Moscow's thriving black market for more than half the monthly salary of a typical worker. Young people speak openly with foreigners about their desire to travel, to see the world.

Abdalov

Shalamov   Shalamov

Moscow courtyard

Young Pioneers march through Red Square in the annual parade.

Though every Soviet child receives military training in school, few take it as seriously as these boys from the Suvorov Military School.

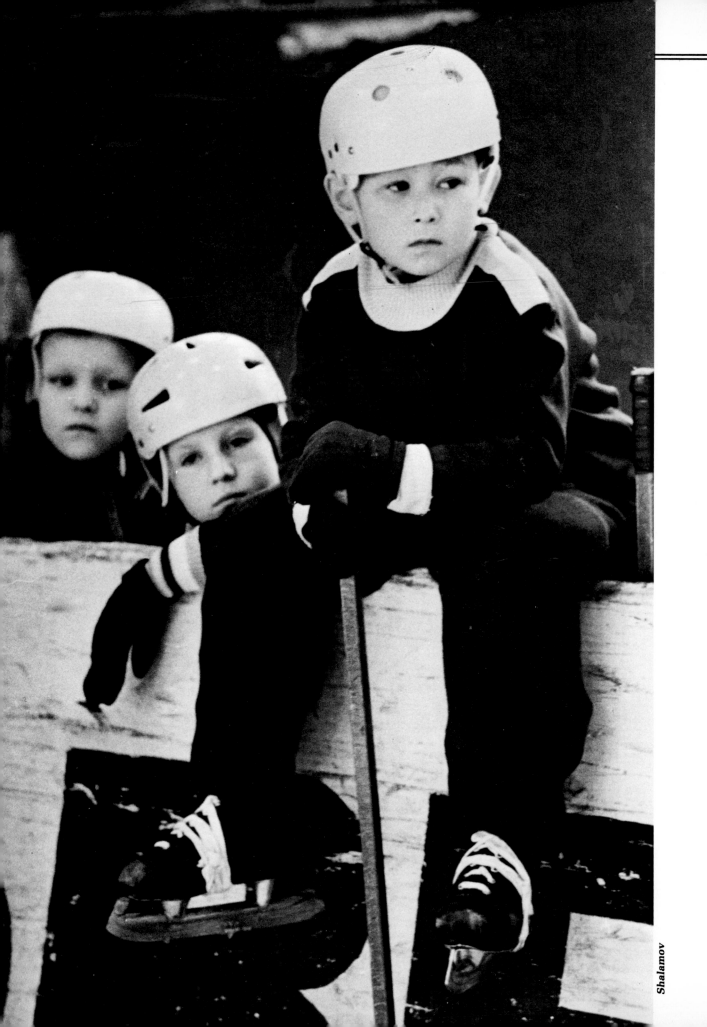

These serious students of ice hockey play for a team sponsored by the Central Army Sports Club, one of the country's huge sports organizations that train Soviet athletes in many fields. In 1945 almost no one in Russia played ice hockey. Today the Russians are probably the best hockey players in the world.

Hull

Moscow schoolgirls. The girl on the left is wearing her school uniform and the scarf of the Young Pioneers.

But young people learn to go along with the system, too. They learn the benefits of keeping up in school, taking part in the regular political lessons, joining and working in the Young Pioneers and then the Young Communist League. Relatively sophisticated youngsters in Moscow or Leningrad learn to put up with all this even if it strikes them personally as silly. Few young people seem to question the basic way things work.

Russians are proud of the strength of their family ties. The family suffers or exults together at important moments for individual family members. Perhaps the best example of this is the collective struggle to win admission to college. In a student's last year of secondary school, the entire family concentrates on the series of oral exams which must be passed to win a place in a university or institute. That year the family's summer plans will depend entirely on the applicant's fate: "If he passes

Different generations in Kiev.

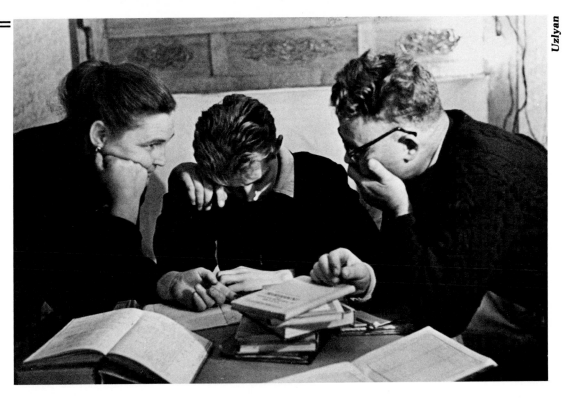

A family discussion about poor marks in school.

Students are given tours of factories and enterprises, many of which are always eager to hire young workers.

The medical institute at Kazan is typical of the huge schools that produce Soviet doctors after just six years of training, directly from high school. The Russians both teach and practice medicine on a mass scale, giving the country a large number of physicians whose training does not satisfy a rigorous western standard.

the university exams in July, we'll have a holiday in August. But if he fails the July exam, we'll have to prepare for the institute exams in August."

Admission to university is one of the many situations in Soviet life where a little *blat* can go a long way. *Blat* is the Russian word for influence or connections. *Blat* at the university might be a friend on the faculty who could put in a good word. (Because all the entrance exams are oral, fixing the results is relatively easy.) *Blat* with the local Communist party committee might also help a family get a private apartment or a paid vacation on the Black Sea.

There is room in the country's educational institutes and universities for about a quarter of the secondary school graduates. The rest go to work. Many get married right out of school. Most of the marriages now performed in Moscow involve brides and grooms who are both under twenty.

The entrance exam for the Leningrad Institute of Art.

Students can be assigned to summer jobs far from home. These young men from the Kharkov Institute of Aviation are helping to build a road in Siberia.

Shalamov

Gluck

Kaspiev

Tulchinsky

A young couple quaffs a pint of Kvass, a soft drink made from dark Russian bread, before their wedding.

Uzlyan

Registering a marriage.

Abdalov

This *Volga* automobile has been decorated to serve in a Moscow wedding. The doll is a new Russian tradition, attached to the car that carries the bride and groom to symbolize their future offspring. On a Saturday or Sunday the streets around Red Square are often filled with these cars. They are waiting for newlyweds who have come to act out another new tradition by placing flowers at Lenin's tomb immediately after their wedding ceremony.

Wide World Photos

The Palace of Weddings in Leningrad was once a grand private mansion.
The ladies in the foreground represent the state and conduct
the wedding ceremony.

Country wedding.

Poliakov

An impeccable Moscow living room in what the Russians call a "modern" block of flats. The room is characteristic of millions of Soviet apartments. The wooden floor is bare because carpets are so hard to find. At night the sofa is converted into a bed—living rooms are a luxury by Soviet standards. The radio is old-fashioned but the television is new. Now color sets are available, though at very high prices.

The Soviet state has so systematized marriage that it is a simple process. The legal arrangements can be formalized simply by signing the appropriate documents at a neighborhood registry office. Couples who want a ceremony can go to a wedding palace, where marriages are ground out in assembly line fashion, but also in grand surroundings. At Moscow's popular wedding palace, once the mansion of a wealthy merchant, the waiting period for a weekend wedding is three months, though the women civil servants who perform the ceremony routinely do fifty of them a day.

Divorce is even easier than marriage, provided there is no dispute, and Soviet marriages dissolve with great regularity. According to official statistics, more than a third of all marriages end in divorce—a source of official anxiety. Articles have been published in the press suggesting why this happens.

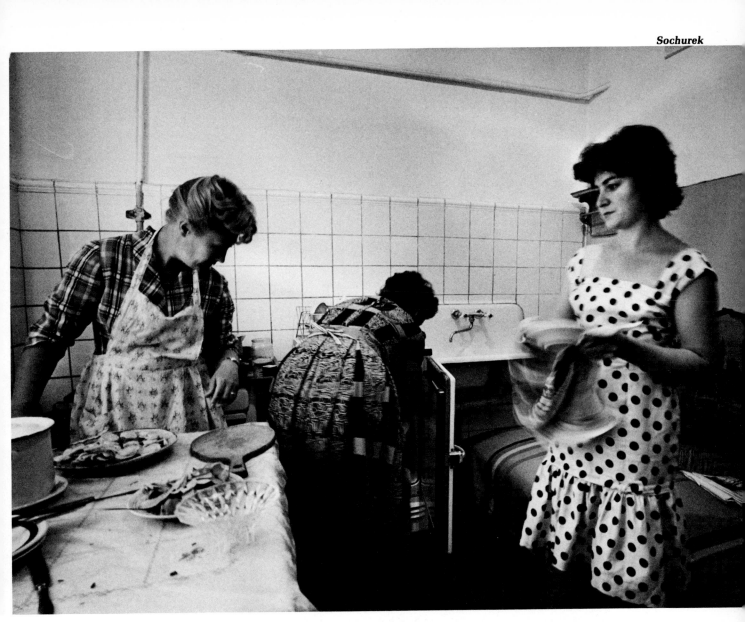

The kitchen of the same flat—equipped with an extra bed. Kitchen gadgetry is still rare. Refrigerators can be found in less than half the country's households, and they are tiny. Blenders, mixers, garbage disposals, and dishwashers are all unheard of.

"Accelerated sexual development does not run parallel with social development," one expert on family psychology wrote in a Soviet newspaper. Her readers would have readily understood the reference to the willingness of Soviet youngsters to experiment sexually in their adolescent years. "Young people do not have the sufficient psychological maturity," the same article went on. "Our children . . . haven't yet encountered questions of the family budget, housekeeping, or a husband's role in domestic duties."

The large number of divorces is one of many factors contributing to a low and still-declining birthrate in European Russia that alarms the Soviet authorities. The total population of the Soviet Union continues to grow briskly, thanks to the high fertility rate in non-Russian parts of the country, partic-

Poliakov

Palmin

The Leningrad Housing Exchange. There are informal housing markets like this one in every Soviet city. The notices posted on the wall announce rooms for rent, apartments to swap or share. Once allocated by the authorities, an apartment is virtually a private possession. But it is possible to rent out space privately or to swap. For example, a couple getting a divorce might try to swap a two-room flat with two young people who each have a room and are getting married. In the background is a typical Soviet apartment house.

ularly in Central Asia. Ethnic Russians now make up barely half the total population of the USSR, but because they are reproducing so slowly, the non-Russian Soviet peoples could become a substantial majority in the foreseeable future.

Young couples in the Russian towns and cities who have more than a single child are exceptional. The parents seem to feel that the hardships imposed by larger families—in terms of the mother's lost time at work, the extra chores at home, the cost and the infringement on scarce living space—outweigh the pleasures of a big family.

Breakfast in a rural cottage, where an icon looks over the household.

Joseloff   Ogden

A crowd at "GUM," Moscow's principal department store.

Shopping for neckties. The sales staff has been instructed to wear masks because of a flu epidemic.

A place to live looms large in Soviet life. Lenin himself ordained that every citizen is entitled to ten square meters—about ninety-eight square feet—of living space, not counting kitchen, bathroom, or hallways. That amounts to one room ten feet square, but the norm has never been met, despite a continuing, extensive program of new apartment construction.

Newly married couples will probably have to move in with parents, perhaps stay with them for years while waiting for a place of their own. More than a fourth of the country's urban population still lives in shared, communal quarters or dormitories; so a personal flat—even for a large extended family—is one of the prizes of Soviet life. Some of the closeness of Soviet families may be dictated more by the need to share living space than by sheer affection.

Kaspiev

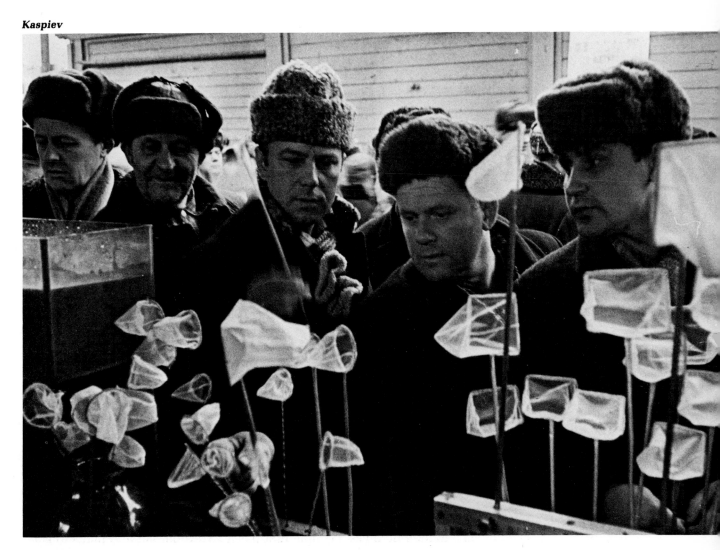

The Moscow pet market, a popular tourist attraction as well as a busy marketplace for fish, birds, dogs, and cats.

The typical modern Soviet apartment is a modest affair. One or two small rooms is the norm; three or more is rare. The design is strictly functional, and includes a kitchen, bathroom, and separate small closet for the toilet. Most new housing being built now is in high-rise buildings in huge "microregions" on the edges of established cities—sprawling developments that can go on for miles.

By capitalist standards, Soviet housing is cheap. Rents are heavily subsidized by the state, and some cooperative apartments are sold at affordable prices. The average urban family probably spends no more than 20 percent of its income on housing, including all utilities. Occupancy is as good as ownership, and a desirable apartment will be passed from generation to generation like a family estate.

A Moscow capitalist. This woman is selling seeds at one of Moscow's many farmers' markets, where villagers can sell the produce from their legal (and tiny) private plots. These private plots are a constant reminder of the failure of collectivized agriculture, and also a tribute to the spirit of free enterprise that survives more than sixty years after the Bolshevik Revolution. Private plots cover about 3 percent of the country's cultivated land, and provide more than 30 percent of the Soviet Union's food.

The authorities permit citizens to swap apartments among themselves, and a thriving unofficial market has developed. The typical situation involves a couple that has a two-room flat and plans to get divorced. This pair would ideally like to find another couple that is just getting married, each of whom has a one-room flat that he or she would like to swap. (Because of the housing shortage, divorced couples often must continue living together.) Or a family that has "inherited" a *babushka*'s one room might want to swap that and its present flat for something bigger or better-located. Every big city has an outdoor "market" where notices of apartments wanted or available for trade can be posted. A large, unofficial real estate industry also exists in the person of illegal operators who undertake to solve housing problems for a fat fee.

Winter scene in a Moscow farmers' market. The lady on the left with the fur collar is a member of Moscow's bourgeoisie, and apparently an assiduous shopper who scours the city's markets.

An ice-cream stand in Moscow.

A Soviet advertisement: "Good vision is a help on the job!" The sign is a good indication of how far Soviet experiments with advertising have come.

Shopping for furniture can be a long-term proposition. The models on display here are probably available to be ordered, not purchased on the spot, and it may be six months or a year before the order is filled.

The average Soviet worker earns about 150 rubles a month.

A fashion show—workers' fashions, on display for a white-collar audience. Whether the workclothes being shown will ever be manufactured and sold is problematical. Moscow's House of Fashion is famous for putting on shows of dresses and suits of which just one copy has been—or will be—made.

A typical Russian family spends many hours every week on the most basic tasks, first of all shopping. Shopping is an art in the Soviet Union, at least for those who want to find more than the most basic items of nourishment and clothing. Many Russians *do* live in utter simplicity, eating only readily available foods—milk products, potatoes, bread, salami, cabbage—and wearing a basic, unchanging wardrobe. But increasingly, Russians are seeking out better things—the *embourgeoisement* of the Soviet Union is proceeding apace. Seeking out better things is a big job, however, requiring ingenuity, good luck, and great patience.

Russians ordinarily carry a "just in case bag" with them all the time—just in case they happen across some desirable product for sale as they move about town. A good shopper will jump into a queue wherever he or she finds it, taking a place and then asking what is being offered for sale at the other end. It might be a shipment of oranges from Morocco or copies of a popular book on Ukrainian herbal medicine.

The queue is ubiquitous in Soviet life, and it comes in many forms. The queue to buy a private car may be five years long, and a purchaser must pay the full price before joining the line. (A car costs about five years salary for an average worker.) Members of the Union of Writers in Moscow have been known to stay in line for ten days to buy a rare edition of an important book. Mothers will spend an entire day at the Children's World department store hoping to buy an aluminum sled for winter. At the neighborhood bread store, three lines are not uncommon: one to make a selection, another to pay the cashier, a third to exchange the cashier's receipt for the chosen loaf.

As a rule, domestic chores are unequally shared within the family. Mama is expected to do a lion's share of the shopping and cooking, cleaning and laundry. (Most families still do their laundry by hand in a bathtub or sink, so it is a big job.) According to Soviet sociologists, younger couples share the housework more fairly than their parents, but it is a rare Soviet household in which the husband does not play the role of king of the castle. "Sometimes," a Russian comedian jokes in a popular skit, "papa helps out after supper by turning on the television."

On a more formal level, Soviet women have been "liberated." Nearly all women work, and a wide range of career opportunities are open to them. (There is no woman member of the politburo, however—women can be doctors, not leaders.) In fact, Soviet careerwomen who must also be housekeepers are constantly torn between the two roles. Absenteeism by mothers is common; both bosses and

Escalators carry passengers to and from the Moscow Metro. The sign says "Exit to street and transfer point" to another subway line.

Sandler

These young men all live in the new city of Togliattigrad and work in the giant automobile plant the Soviet Union purchased from Fiat of Italy. Here they are waiting for a city bus to take them to work.

That Fiat factory and other investments in the automotive industry have brought the Soviet Union into its own automobile age. Now theft is a serious problem—the theft of entire cars and, more commonly, theft of individual parts by car owners who cannot buy what they need in the hopelessly disorganized official spare parts network. The lock on this car door is indicative, and the missing windshield wipers are normal. Drivers routinely keep those easily stolen and impossible-to-replace treasures inside their cars, except when it rains.

At the beauty parlor.

On the telephone in Tallinn.

Abdalov

Everyday excitement.

colleagues assume that mothers will take time away from their jobs to shop, care for sick children, and so on.

Mothers and grandmothers traditionally provide the adhesive that holds Russian families together, and when they do it well the result is a monument to human will and emotion. A tightly knit Russian family is a fortress that protects all within from the strains and uncertainties of life outside.

The best of family life can be seen at important celebrations, a birthday or perhaps New Year's Eve. All the generations gather together; an enormous feast of a dozen or more dishes is prepared; everyone squeezes around the biggest table available (it is never quite big enough) for a long evening of toasts, jokes, eating and drinking. There is no formality involved, no fine china and silverware, no coffee and cognac after dinner in the living room (no living room). And anyone who has shared one of these evenings knows that there could be no better party.

A big family celebration provides a natural outlet for Russian emotionalism, a boundless national resource. Russians love to hug and kiss, weep and wail in grief, make grand gestures in love or friendship (a distinction Russians would not understand). Russians are masters at generating human warmth, and they need no more elaborate setting than a kitchen table to perform this act of creativity.

Indeed, sitting around a small kitchen table is a basic Russian pastime. Kitchen tables may be the single most important tangible goods in the lives of many Russians, particularly the country's intellectuals. Russians call them "the intelligentsia," and they are an extraordinary group of people.

The modern Soviet system is not designed for the satisfaction of intellectuals. The regime is ideologically rigid, afraid of new ideas, compelled to censor everything that is published. Despite these constraints—or perhaps because of them—the intelligentsia survives, even thrives in small corners of the society, particularly in Moscow and Leningrad.

Poliakov

Andrei Voznesensky, one of the Soviet Union's most popular poets, reads his verses to an audience of more than 10,000 in a Moscow ice-hockey stadium. Poetry and poets are extremely popular in the USSR. Someone like Voznesensky is the equivalent of a matinée idol. His books of poems sell out literally in hours, and strangers constantly stop him on the street.

Culture for the masses—a symphony orchestra plays inside a factory for the workers.

Uzlyan

Moscow's intellectuals are a special category of the Soviet population. Their faces seem familiar to a western eye, as do their interests and concerns. These are artists gathered for a discussion of sculpture in Moscow's House of Artists.

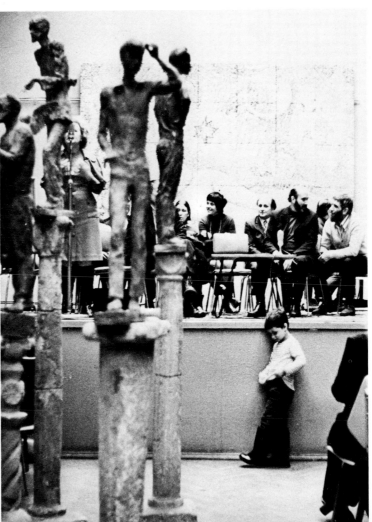

A Soviet intellectual likes nothing better than "a real Russian conversation," which is likely to mean an intense, prolonged discussion of virtually every question that comes to mind, from the existence of God to the chronic shortage of coffee. There is only one proper setting for a real Russian conversation—around the kitchen table.

Intellectuals lead different lives than ordinary Russians. They share the physical circumstances of modern Soviet life, but the best of them are engaged in a constant struggle over ideas that sets them apart from working-class compatriots. A good theater director is likely to be waging constant battle with the Ministry of Culture over the plays he would like to produce. A good writer is always struggling with the censors. A good scholar worries that political considerations will prevent him from writing what he knows or saying what he thinks. These struggles become the central focus of daily life. Soviet intellectuals who have emigrated in recent years discover that the theoretical freedom they can find in Israel or America is not always a satisfactory substitute for the intensity of their old lives in the USSR.

Of course there is a corrupted Soviet intelligentsia too—intellectuals who have totally abandoned any personal standards in order to please the authorities and win whatever benefits for themselves that they can. Such people generally rise to the top of the Soviet intellectual establishment. They become the sparring partners for the many more honest people who try to do something truthful or creative within the system.

Russians love their time off, whether an afternoon or a month's vacation (to which every citizen is entitled).

The Russian word for a day off means, literally, "a going-out day," and there is nothing Russians like better than just going out into the woods or fields to commune with nature. On weekends, Moscow's many railroad stations are filled with citizens who are taking trains into the countryside for a day of hunting mushrooms, swimming, cross-country skiing, or whatever the weather permits.

Less adventurous souls might spend an afternoon at the race track, where the state makes book (at horrendously unfavorable odds), as do a number of unofficial bookmakers. Another popular entertainment is the public baths, an old Russian tradition that seems to be surviving the era of private

Uzlyan Antsis

A day in the woods. △

A motorcycle club. ▽

Skiing through a Russian Winter.

Uzlyan

**A Sunday outing to the World War II memorial
at Volgograd, formerly Stalingrad.**

apartments and private bathrooms. One buys bunches of birch leaves on the way into the bath to
swat out the grime while sizzling in the hot, dry heat.

A night on the town generally means a movie, play, or concert. Russians boast constantly of their
devotion to "culture," and indeed almost any kind of public spectacle is guaranteed to draw a crowd.
Every medium-sized city has regular live theater, and probably has its own symphony orchestra too,
though the quality of neither is high. The best—by far the best—theater and music can be found in
Moscow and Leningrad, both of which maintain great Russian traditions in the performing arts. It is a
point of official pride, however, that even the best attractions should be brought occasionally to citizens who live far from the two major cities. When Mstislav Rostropovich got into trouble with the

**Rugby players. The poster is a quotation from Lenin: "In our laboring country we need an army of
millions of physically strong people. . . ."**

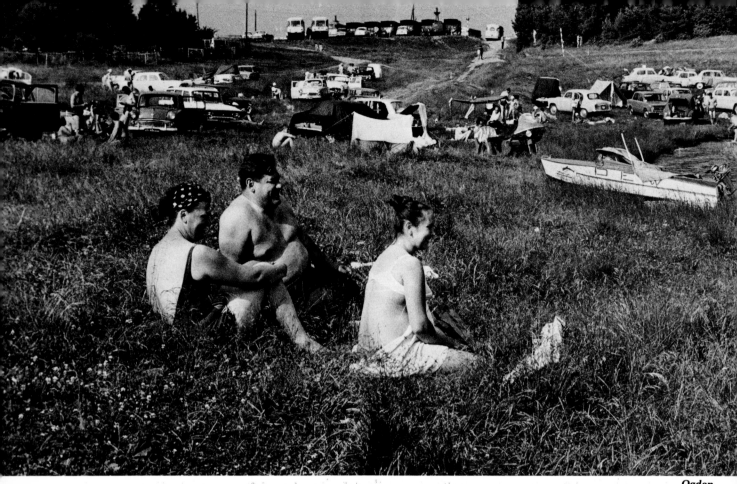

Muscovites taking the sun at a broad spot on a river just outside the capital that is called the "Bay of Joys."

authorities some years ago, he was denied permission to play his cello outside the USSR, and was sent instead on a concert tour of remote Siberian towns.

Restaurants and cafés provide a venue for another sort of night on the town, though Russians themselves complain about the paucity and poor quality of these enterprises. A restaurant may be the best single example of the drawbacks of state socialism; without an entrepreneurial boss who is anxious to please his clients, a restaurant cannot easily rise above the level of a cafeteria with waiters. Nevertheless, the establishments that do exist are usually crowded, particularly on weekends, and there

The Russians call this "four on a bottle," and it is a sign of Soviet-style inflation. When vodka was cheaper, three men traditionally shared a half-liter bottle, but price increases have pushed that up to four. The man whose back is to the camera is holding the bottle. It will take them five to ten minutes to finish it all.

Poliakov

Abdalov

Poliakov

seems a great demand for places to go to eat, drink, and dance. A proper restaurant will h
chestra of some sort, perhaps just an accordion player and drummer, perhaps a group of y
ple with electric guitars and a strong desire to play like western pop musicians. The c
happily dance the night away. And if the men drink too much, as they often do, the wom
be embarrassed to dance with each other.

Young workers too fond of vodka hear lectures on the evils of drink.

The Russian word for a vacation is also suggestive; it means a "letting go," and this is just what a Russian thinks the purpose of a proper holiday should be. Let go of ordinary concerns, and sometimes of ordinary restraints, too.

Fortunate citizens find places in government-subsidized rest homes and sanatoriums for their

Komar and Melamid

This is a scene from an official filmstrip on the dangers of alcoholism. The men have all been picked up drunk by the police and taken to a drying-out station, where they are now hearing this lecture.

month's vacation. These establishments appeal to the pampered child that seems to survive in many Russians. They require no effort to enjoy. But husbands and wives are unlikely to get invited to the same establishment at the same time, since invitations are handed out at work, and only for individual visits. Families that want to vacation together might travel to the Black Sea coast where they can live in a campground or rent beds in the apartments of local residents, a thriving and legal form of free enterprise in resort areas. Many Russians choose to go nowhere at all, preferring to take their month off at home in one concentrated loaf.

Much Russian time off is devoted to drinking vodka, or recovering from that activity. This has been a Russian weakness for at least a thousand years. Alcoholism is the Soviet Union's most serious social problem. It costs the state billions of rubles each year in days lost from work, illness, accidents, crime, and more. The authorities propagandize intensively against the evils of drinking, to no apparent avail.

Stalin permitted the Russian Orthodox church to train thousands of priests during World War II, when the church actively supported the war effort. That generation is now dying out, and the church has been unable to train as many young men.

But the state also depends on vodka as a source of revenue. The distilling industry is highly profitable, and the taxes on vodka and wine sales bring in a large fraction of the national budget. This is literally a dilemma without a solution.

Russians have their own way of drinking. The sociable cocktail before dinner is not a familiar custom. Russians drink as they eat, chasing great gulps of vodka with morsels of food, or they drink simply to get drunk in a hurry. People complain that they cannot keep vodka around their apartments,

Churchgoers crowd into Mocow's largest Baptist church. Soviet Baptists continue to proselytize and thrive despite constant tensions with the authorities.

Jews outside the synagogue in Kiev, where the Jewish community is at least 1,000 years old.

because it seems inevitably to get drunk up if it is available. Perhaps the most revealing fact about Russian vodka is the way it is packaged. Each bottle has a top made of heavy aluminum foil; once the top is removed, it cannot be replaced.

Vodka offers one way to escape from everyday life; religion offers another—and it may be nearly as popular. Despite more than sixty years of official atheism, Russian Orthodoxy still thrives in Russia. Many other religions have managed to stay alive and sometimes to prosper.

Religion is one of many interesting aspects of contemporary Soviet life on which no statistics are published, but Orthodox priests will tell you that 30 to 50 million Russians consider themselves believers. (The Soviet population includes about 130 million Russians and an equal number of other nationalities and races.) Certainly regular churchgoers outnumber the Communist party's 15 million members. Parents who claim to be disinterested still find time to have their children baptized, and the emotional and intellectual force of Eastern Orthodox Christianity is still tangible in contemporary Soviet life. The Orthodox church is also a link to the prerevolutionary Russian past, an important reason for its continuing appeal.

The overwhelming majority of people in church on an ordinary Sunday morning are older women, but this is probably no more significant in Russia than it is in Rome or Madrid where the same is true. In fact, young people do take part in the church, in growing numbers according to some priests.

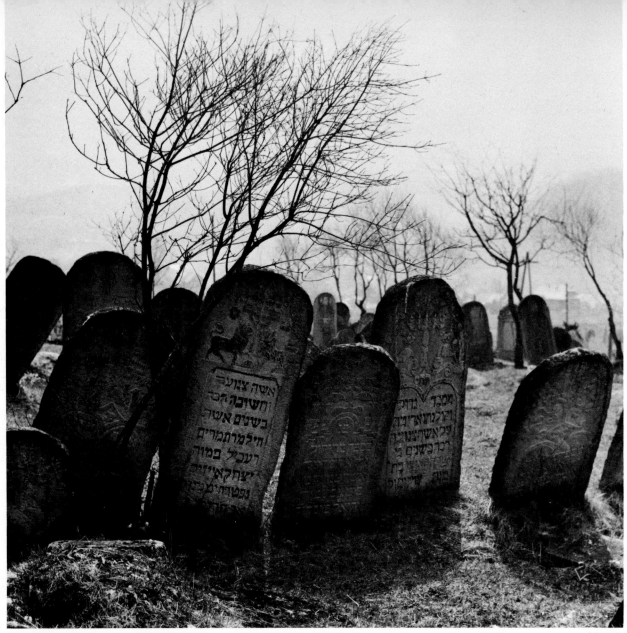

Antsis

A Jewish cemetery in the Ukraine.

Other faiths enjoy less official tolerance. The Jewish religion has been all but obliterated in the Soviet Union, though many who were born into Jewish families retain a sense of Jewish identity. Roman Catholicism remains strong in Lithuania, partly as an expression of local nationalism. Islam survives in Central Asia, though it has been buffeted by the modernizing influences of Soviet power in that region. The Baptist religion is surprisingly strong in Russia and the Ukraine—a bible-thumping, rhythmic, and intense strain familiar to anyone who has traveled in the American South. Despite harassment from the authorities, the Baptists are proselytizing and even building new churches.

The fact that religion can still thrive demonstrates the true nature of the Soviet dictatorship. This is not Orwell's *1984*, where even thoughts could be controlled. On the contrary, the Soviet authorities have had to make room for all sorts of unofficial, even antiofficial activities. Religion is perhaps the best single example. The rituals of Russian Orthodoxy, like the Hebrew language and Moslem prayers, are passed on from one to another outside any official channel, but they survive. There is

To market in a Volga village.

also a huge unofficial economy, in which tradesmen provide services "on the left," in the Russian phrase—outside the state-run economic system. Russians who are determined to avoid Marxism-Leninism and the trappings of the state in their own lives can do so, provided they don't try to offer any alternative political program of their own.

If there is a surviving physical link to old Russia, it is the countryside. The Soviet years have transformed rural life at least in an organizational sense, but many aspects of peasant life seem to remain constant. A popular school of contemporary writers has produced a number of books and plays about the countryside that suggest a romantic appreciation for something that is more Russian than Soviet.

Village lunch break.

It is probably more difficult for the people who actually live in the countryside to romanticize rural Russian life, which remains poor and backward. A third of the Soviet population still lives in rural areas. The authorities are anxious to preserve that ratio to ensure adequate manpower to work the collective and state farms. But even the authorities acknowledge that amenities in the villages fall far short of modern standards. Implicitly, they also admit that given a free choice, many peasants would flee the farms. But peasants who work on the state and collective farms are not issued the "internal passports" or identity cards that are required for travel around the country. Without passports they are effectively bound to the land.

Even Russians who live in the big cities marvel at the differences between their lives and those of the modern peasantry. Electricity is still far from universal in the countryside, and the consumer goods available in rural stores—from food and clothing to more exotic fare—are very inferior to what is available in the larger cities. Many farmers depend on the produce of their tiny but legal private plots to provide basic nourishment for their families.

Sichov

The village store.

Sochurek

A village on the banks of the Volga on the day supplies are delivered.

The private plots invariably get more attention than the fields of the collective farms. (In the country as a whole, these plots account for roughly 3 percent of the cultivated land, but provide—through a network of farmers' markets in towns and cities—more than a fourth of the total food supply.)

The countryside is organized into huge collective or state farms that may include thousands of people. A big farm has its own Party organization, local governing authority, clinic, schools, and some-

Making lunch.

times even some light industry such as food processing. But the organizational structure has barely altered the basic flavor of rural life, which seems remarkably unchanged over many years.

Some big farms are now building blocks of flats for their workers, but peasants still seem to favor the traditional wooden cottage, preferably with carved wooden trim.

Feeding the cows.

The Stalin tattoo was popular during World War II.

Gluck

A family from the provinces in Moscow. Citizens from the provinces flood the capital—a million of them every day, according to official estimate—to sightsee and shop for goods that are not available at home.

Rural folk still count on the Orthodox priest to perform the basic rituals of life, from baptism to funeral. They still respect ancient folkways and superstitions, and still brew their own vodkalike spirits which they consume in great quantity—despite laws forbidding home distilling. According to accounts written by several Moscow intellectuals in recent years, the rural population goes about its business relatively indifferent to the official sloganeering and propagandizing that are central aspects of city life.

A woman tends to her private plot. Gardens this size provide nearly a third of the food eaten in the Soviet Union.

Stalin paid little attention to rural life after his initial collectivization of agriculture, concentrating instead on the industrialization of the country. But in the last thirty years the countryside has been the beneficiary of many government programs and a continuing high rate of investment. Khrushchev boldly opened an arid section of central Asia called the Virgin Lands to increase the amount of tillable land, and this risky experiment has proven a success. In the Brezhnev era the production of farm machinery has grown steadily, and Soviet farms have begun to produce substantial quantities of

A country barber comes to the fields to perform his services during the busy harvest.

Uzlyan

Stone

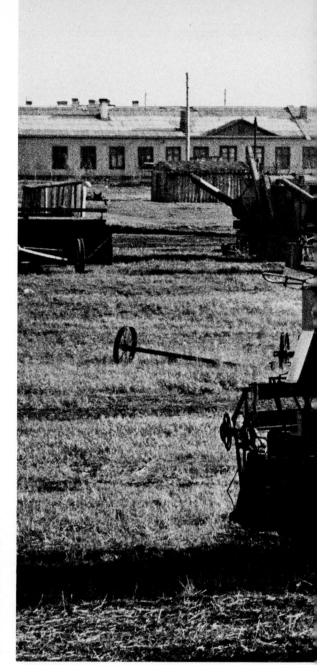

Maintenance of machinery is a chronic problem on the collective farms. These machines are all out of order.

The leadership constantly exhorts the rural population to adopt modern methods and become more efficient. This is a young student of tractor-driving who is working in a harvest "on practice," as the Russians put it. The communications system is meant to get the tractors to the places they are most needed.

Sochurek

Uzlyan

meat, though per capita consumption is still relatively low. Average levels of agricultural production continue to rise, but erratic results and chronic inefficiency remain the norm. Wild fluctuations in the size of the harvest from year to year can have devastating effects on the entire Soviet economy, although the government has found it can prevent wholesale famine by importing vast quantities of grain.

Russian tradition dictates respect for old age, and this tradition also survives. The hyperactive cultures of the capitalist world have found old people to be a bother, an embarrassment. Russians make room for their old if they can.

Gathering wood for winter.

Siberian winter. The animals are reindeer.

Kaspiev

This doesn't make old age any great pleasure though. It is still lonely and boring, and the state has not yet done a great deal to help. Pensions are modest, and the medical system does not concentrate on the problems of the elderly. In fact, there is no geriatrics specialty in Soviet medicine at all, and nursing homes for the old are uncommon. Old people without families to take care of them are often thrown back on their own devices. A popular hangout for the elderly in Moscow is the music conservatory, where pensioners can listen to student recitals.

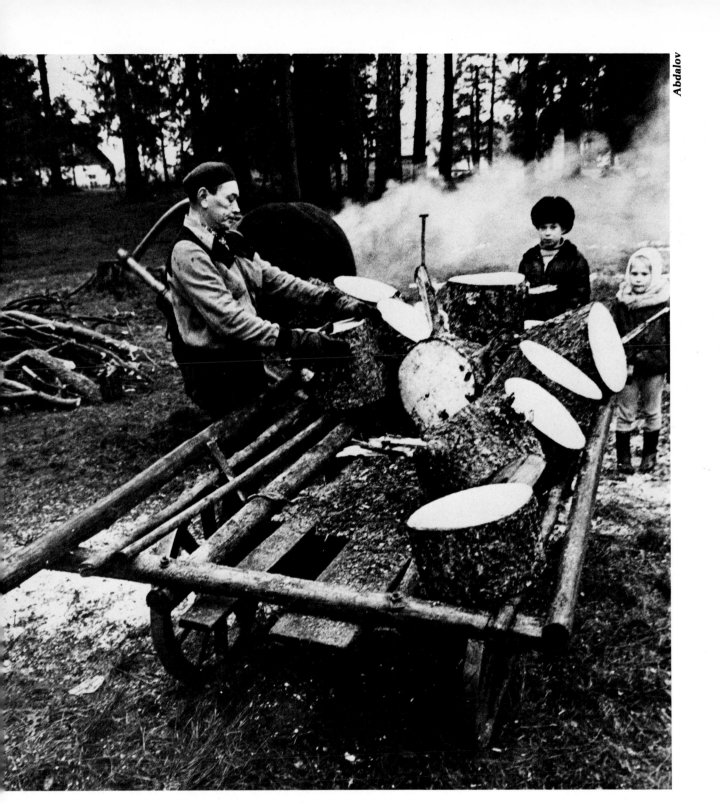

Abdalov

Most Russians die at home. Soviet hospitals encourage relatives to take terminal patients to their own rooms or apartments rather than fill a hospital bed—and depersonalize the last days of life. Even persons dying of cancer are left at home; doctors visit regularly but there is no pretext of intensive professional care.

Burial, like marriage, is one of the traditional church functions now performed by the state. Every

The village doctor. This young woman grew up in the village that helped finance her medical education. Now she is the only doctor in the area, and in return for her modest salary (less than the earnings of many industrial workers) she ministers as best she can to a remote population. The village has its own small clinic, but serious cases must be flown to the nearest city.

Uzlyan

Uzlyan

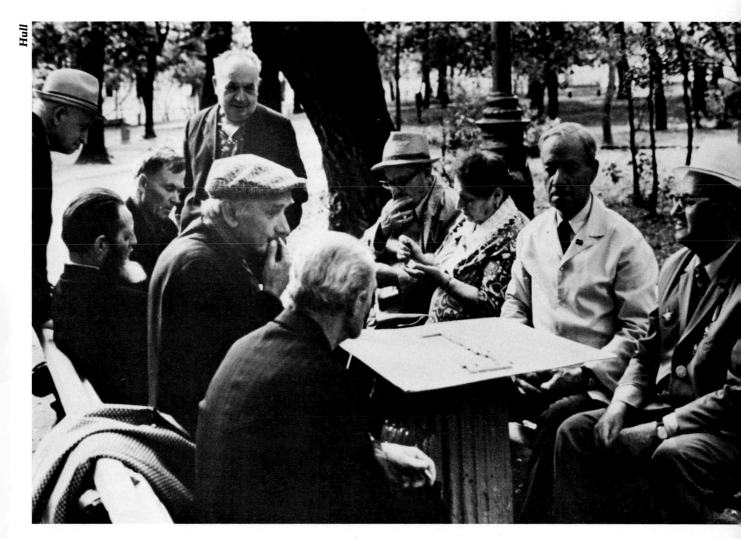

Dominoes in a Moscow park.

Babushka and grandson fueled by a supply of cole slaw, ride the train to town.
Those who live on the farms are not given internal passports, the document
needed to travel freely around the country. To take a trip, then, one must have
a formal letter approving it from an official of the collective farm organization.
Without a passport, a villager cannot move to a town or city to take an
industrial job. These controls help the authorities maintain the rural
population, which is still about 30 percent of the total.

Hull

Babushki

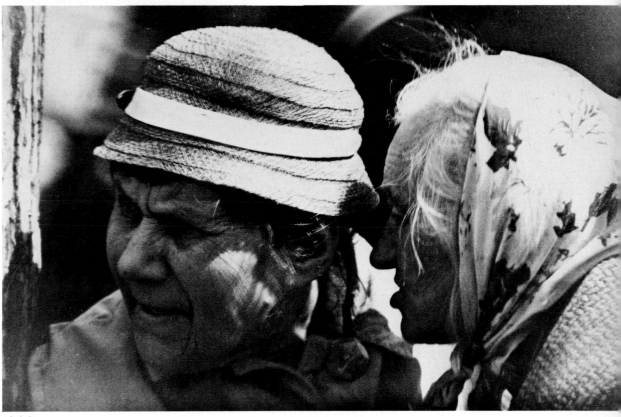

Abdalov

The photograph is of Vladimir Komarov, a Soviet cosmonaut
who was killed in a space accident. His remains have just been
buried here in the Kremlin wall, and his wife is mourning in
traditional Russian fashion.

Abdalov

Shalamov

Minding the cemetery.

city has a crematorium where families can take their dead for a secular funeral service. The Moscow crematorium on the edge of the city is a big marble box. It has three chapellike rooms inside, each of them with one wall of glass that overlooks a pleasant rural scene. A funeral can last exactly thirty minutes; then the mourners must make room for another party. It is up to the family to organize some sort of service. Russians like to see their dead one last time; so open coffins are common. Loud crying and mourning are not discouraged.

After a funeral at the Moscow crematorium, the family of the deceased is invited to return in a week for an urn of ashes. These can be buried in an ordinary cemetery, in a special memorial wall, or they can be taken home. Many families buy cemetery plots, surround them with an iron fence, and mark the grave with the distinctive Russian Orthodox cross.

THE NATIONAL

ICON

Vladimir Ilyich Lenin is the only officially recognized deity in the modern Soviet Union. His image is everywhere; in every government office, every classroom, every village square. Lenin's bald pate and jutting goatee are symbols of the Soviet state.

This deification was Stalin's idea, and it began shortly after Lenin's death in 1924. Lenin's wife and comrade, Nadezhda Krupskaya, published a public plea just nine days after he died: "Do not raise memorials to him, name places after him, hold solemn festivals to commemorate his life, etc. To all this he attached so little importance in his life; all this was so burdensome to him. . . ." Her request could not have been more thoroughly ignored.

Stalin obviously sensed Lenin's symbolic value. In the brief period of his rule, Lenin established himself in the public imagination as a giant figure. He was the personification of the Revolution, an event that would never have taken place without his own daring and resolve. In life his role as supreme leader was virtually unquestioned. So Stalin decided to enshrine Lenin as a symbol of the legitimacy of Bolshevik rule over Russia. Several years later, when Stalin had established himself firmly as Lenin's successor, he began to order the rewriting of the history of the revolution, placing himself at Lenin's side at events in the early 1900s when, in fact, the two barely knew one another.

Today Lenin is ubiquitous. Two- and three-year-olds in nurseries and kindergartens are taught "to recognize V. I. Lenin in portraits and illustrations," in the words of a teacher's manual. At age six schoolchildren are taken to their town's Lenin monument to lay a wreath on the founder's birthday. Children's books preach the gospel of Lenin. In one especially ingenious tale written for second graders, a little boy pleads to be allowed to go hunting in the forest with the grownups. The older men say no, he is too little to hunt. The boy is devastated. But then another man appears, a man who looks like Lenin himself and who is called Ilyich, Lenin's nickname. The newcomer speaks up for the boy: He can take care of himself, this Ilyich says, so let the lad go on the hunt. The boy is thrilled.

The Soviet public today is clearly smitten with the image of Lenin. Thousands of Russians wait in a long, meandering queue almost every day of the year to see the waxen figure in a glass box that is said to be Lenin himself, and which lies in the famous tomb on Red Square. Young couples, while still in their wedding suits and gowns, can often be seen on the square laying flowers beside the tomb; it is thought to bring good luck to go there directly from the wedding palace.

A poster of the founding father dominates a Moscow façade.

Lenin in a barber-shop window …

Soviet citizens wait in line for a glimpse of Lenin's preserved remains which lie in the depths of the mausoleum on Red Square.

... and presiding over a typical cloakroom in a Soviet office building.

114

Virtually every city, town, and village has its own Lenin square.

Nisnevich

Shalamov

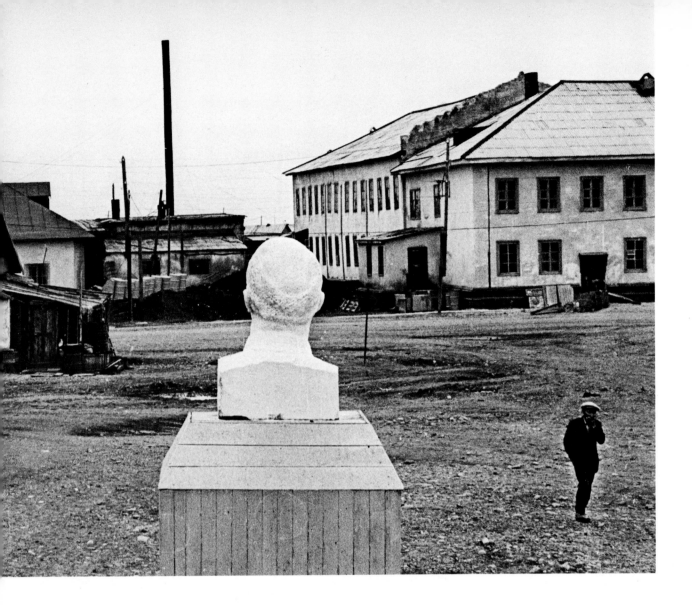

Lenin's name is now a universal symbol of authority. The regime describes (and thus implicitly justifies) its foreign policy as a *Leninist* foreign policy; workers who behave well are those who respect *Leninist* norms. Scholars know that they are expected to cite one of Lenin's many works in each of their articles and books, no matter how irrelevant the actual citation. The article in the *Great Soviet Encyclopedia* on World War II (which began fifteen years after Lenin died) is followed by a bibliography; its first reference is to *The Collected Works of V. I. Lenin.*

The cult of Lenin is sustained by a steady stream of new books, plays, films, sculpture, and paintings of or about him. Actors who portray the founder on stage earn two or three times their normal salaries. A screenwriter in Kiev who wrote a script about Lenin's family was paid four times his usual royalty. Employees of the Lenin Museum in Moscow (every important city has its Lenin Museum) enjoy the exalted status of employees of the Central Committee of the Communist party. They can use the Central Committee's cafeteria.

In old Russia every family had its icon, a small religious painting of a holy figure who was meant to watch over the household. Today Lenin has become a great national icon, in many ways a substitute for the original version.

THE PARTY AND

THE PROCESS

Outwardly the Soviet system looks familiar. It includes a constitution; an elected parliament; courts and laws; an elaborate government of ministries, councils, and committees. But this is form, not substance. In fact, the Soviet Union is a dictatorship ruled by a tiny band of communists who claim to dictate on behalf of the masses. The autocrats in control can overrule constitution, parliament, ministers, judges, and laws whenever they choose.

Those autocrats are the elders of the Communist party, members of the politburo that rules the land. This is the Party established by Vladimir Ilyich Lenin, and today's Party leaders consider themselves Lenin's heirs. The source of their power is not their formal hold on the official state institutions, but their control over Lenin's Bolshevik party.

The idea that a political party is more important than the governmental apparatus of the state is not easily grasped by westerners. But that is the state of affairs in the USSR. The country's most important leader is the general secretary of the Communist party, not the premier or president (the same man has often held more than one of these positions). The Party's politburo—which is literally the executive committee of the Party Central Committee—is the forum for deciding all important questions of domestic and foreign policy. In the Soviet Republics (the Ukraine, Lithuania, Armenia, Uzbekistan, etc.) there are local governments, but they are subservient to the local branch of the Communist party. The first secretary of the Uzbek Communist party is the most important man in Uzbekistan. Even in a factory, the director—who reports to a ministry in Moscow or in the capital of his republic—only manages day-to-day affairs, while the enterprise's Party secretary retains ultimate responsibility. Soviet courts of law—theoretically divorced entirely from the Party hierarchy—reliably mete out whatever justice Party authorities request.

The Russians refer to these arrangements as "the leading role of the Party." It is the basic fact of Soviet life. Ambitious young people learn at an early age that advancement to the highest levels of Soviet society is unlikely to be open to any but Party members. Many obviously join out of self-interest rather than conviction. There are about 15 million Party members in the population of 260 million.

The Soviets describe their system as "socialist democracy," a choice of words that is likely to confuse an outsider. In fact, the crucial element in the Soviet system is what Lenin called "democratic centralism." That means that "the center"—the politburo—makes all the important decisions. By definition, they are "democratic."

Sovfoto

Twice each year, on November 7 and May 1, the leaders of the Soviet Union gather atop the tomb of Lenin to review a mammoth parade in Red Square. The public is not invited to the parade, except via television. This famous photograph appears on the front page of every newspaper in the country the following day.

While the leaders preside over the Moscow parade, their images are carried through the streets of every provincial capital, at local recreations of the celebration. This is a November 7 parade in Kiev, capital of the Ukraine.

The Supreme Soviet, a parliament whose members are all elected without opposition, and whose votes—like the one being cast here—are invariably unanimous.

This young man is being voted into the Communist party by the Party "collective" in his factory. Peer selection and then peer pressure are meant to maintain Party discipline.

What must be the world's largest marching band strides through Red Square before an audience of invited guests.

The Party's presence is ubiquitous—every office, every enterprise, every farm has a Party secretary. This rugged fellow is the Party secretary on a huge collective farm. Behind him, farm workers are eating lunch served by one of the farm's portable cafés.

A Soviet soldier wraps the red scarf of a Young Pioneer around the neck of this new member. Roughly equivalent to a scout organization, the Pioneers are a Soviet child's first exposure to the Communist party organization. As teenagers, some of them will go on to join the Young Communist League, the stepping stone to membership in the Party itself.

Shalamov   Sochurek

Abdalov

A local Party secretary talks to a group of women who want to hold a religious service in a collapsing old monastery. His mission is to discourage them.

Stalin.

Nisnevich   *Nisnevich*

Nisnevich

Brezhnev.

A classic Soviet official's office, duplicated tens of thousands of times all over the country. An official's importance can often be divined by the size of his portrait of Lenin and the number of telephones on the table behind his desk.

Sochurek

There is a contradiction between appearance and reality that runs throughout the entire Soviet system. Russians are great believers in appearances, and seek to create false ones all the time. So the Soviet constitution promises citizens a wide range of rights and freedoms, but anyone who dares test them can end up in prison. Ask a Soviet official to explain why, and he will point to the qualifying language in the constitution that forbids activities detrimental to the state. So, for example, the theme of every May Day parade through Red Square is the unity of Party and people, leaders and led. But the real public isn't permitted anywhere near Red Square, which is surrounded by cordons of soldiers and police. Inside an elaborate show is staged for the leaders standing atop Lenin's mausoleum, a show of mass acrobatics, mass marching bands, and mass enthusiasm. The enthusiasm is provided by specially chosen representatives of the public who march through the square waving banners and portraits of the leadership. They march through rows and rows of plainclothes police, whose job it is to prevent any hint of spontaneous behavior by the crowd.

The Soviets hold elections for the national parliament, the Supreme Soviet. This body gives unanimous support to every proposal the leaders put before it. There is one candidate for every seat, each one chosen by the authorities in Moscow. No competition is ever permitted, except perhaps the competition between those who declare the official results and their own consciences. According to the official figures, every election for the Supreme Soviet attract a higher percentage of voters than the last. This has been going on so long that the figures have gone far beyond common sense. In 1979, according to the official count, 99.99 percent of the adult population turned out to vote.

What sort of leaders would want to create the impression that they are supported *unanimously* by an enormous population? Certainly not leaders who are confident of their own authority. A strong, confident politician realizes that a certain portion of the public is bound to oppose him no matter what he does. But the men who run the Soviet Union are not self-confident, strong politicians. They reveal their true feelings in their harsh reaction to any hint of organized dissent in the Soviet populace, in their fierce persecution of many religious sects, in their reliance on a gigantic political police force whose principal job is the maintenance of the official orthodoxy. These are the works of insecure leaders, men who have to wonder whether their status as leaders is legitimate.

Soviet leaders achieve their status by pleasing colleagues and superiors, not by winning elections. Popular support is not a serious factor in a Soviet politician's career, but the boss's support is crucial. This one fact explains a great deal about the way Soviet officials behave. An important person whose importance depends only on those *above* him is unlikely to pay much attention to people below. And

An officially released photograph of Leonid Ilyich Brezhnev, then general secretary of the Communist party of the Soviet Union.

that is just what happens in the Soviet Union. The insensitive bureaucrat or Party official is a permanent fixture of Soviet life, one that is even ridiculed in the official press. Equally common is the obsequious official who is trying to flatter his way up the ladder.

Soviet leaders belong to a special caste. Their lives have little in common with those of the ordinary populace. They are cut off by the privileges of rank and power. Ordinary Russians sense this gulf; they refer to their leaders with a slang word (*nachalstvo*) that means, roughly, "the big cheeses." And that is just how they like to behave.

Families of Soviet leaders receive almost no publicity, and the leaders' private lives are meant to have no bearing on their public duties. It is said, that Soviet Premier Alexei Kosygin was informed at the beginning of a May Day parade that his wife had just died. Kosygin stood stoically on top of Lenin's tomb for the next several hours. This is a photograph of Brezhnev's family, released by the government news agency principally for use abroad. It shows *(left to right)* his daughter, mother, grandson, son, and wife.

At the highest level, the two dozen or so full and alternate members of the politburo and the secretaries of the Central Committee of the Party are utterly removed from ordinary Soviet life. They are allocated spacious city apartments, but can often be found in their large country *dachas*. Many of the senior leaders also have hunting lodges along the Volga and big houses on the Black Sea. The leaders ride around in big, chauffeur-driven limousines and are cared for at home by teams of servants. They need never set foot in a normal Soviet shop, but can summon consumer goods that the citizenry never sees. This top sliver of society is said to get its food from a special shop open only to its members; each eligible family pays a nominal monthly fee for an unlimited quantity of foodstuffs, including many choice items that are never sold publicly.

Ernst Neizvestny, a well-known Soviet sculptor, puts final touches on his memorial to Nikita Khrushchev, who had once ridiculed Neizvestny publicly for encouraging experimental young Soviet artists who had strayed from the conventions of Soviet Realism. Khrushchev's family asked Neizvestny to make this marker for his grave, apparently a gesture to the liberal intellectual community as well as an apology to the sculptor himself. The monument Neizvestny designed put the bust of Khrushchev between two intertwined blocks of white and black stone, a metaphor for Khrushchev's career as a Party leader. Khrushchev was buried in a public cemetery that was traditionally a tourist attraction in Moscow. But so many people came to see Khrushchev's grave that the men who deposed him decided the cemetery ought to be closed to the public, and it was.

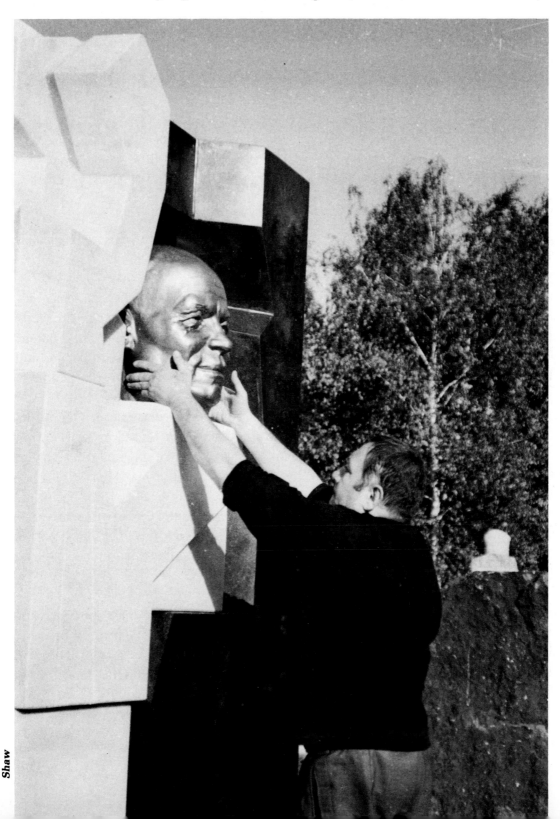

Sochurek

Stalin's daughter, Svetlana Alliluyeva, conveyed the psychology of privilege precisely in one brief anecdote about the late Anastas Mikoyan, a member of the Soviet upper crust for more than forty years:

"At Mikoyan's *dacha*," Svetlana wrote, "even in winter, fresh green vegetables from his own hot-houses were always served. Helping me to some, he once said, 'In the USSR people haven't got the habit of eating green vegetables.' To which I told him that everyone loved green vegetables, but couldn't buy them anywhere.

" 'What are you saying!' exclaimed Mikoyan. 'This year we sold twice as many green vegetables to the people as in any previous year!' "

That anecdote includes another important point about the senior leadership. They are so cut off from real Soviet life that they eventually begin to accept their own propaganda. Perhaps there were official statistics that showed the increase in the sale of vegetables that Mikoyan mentioned, but no one who saw how ordinary Soviet citizens live, even today, could suggest that they had an opportunity to eat many fresh vegetables other than potatoes and cabbage.

The men who run the second superpower are old veterans. All of them came of age in the Stalin era. All of them lived through World War II and know the devastation it caused in Russia. They all helped preside over the great postwar recovery and military development program that transformed the Soviet Union from a devastated backwater into a world power.

Yet they all must share a sense of Russia's persistent inadequacy in many fields, particularly science, technology, and mass production techniques. They know how much remains to be done to make the USSR truly a modern power. They know they are far behind the capitalist world in establishing a comfortable standard of living for their people.

As a general rule, the men at the top come from simple backgrounds in working-class or agricultural families. They are narrowly educated, usually in some technical field, though many of them obviously have good minds—and well-educated assistants. The leaders are not men of the world. In fact, although more and more Russians are visiting foreign countries, the senior leaders (with a few

Some people in the "workers' state" live more like old-fashioned capitalists than workers. These are members of the Academy of Science in Leningrad, relaxing in a parlor of the academy's quarters there, once a grand Petersburg family's private mansion.

A country *Dacha* is one of the greatest privileges bestowed on members of the Soviet elite.
This *Dacha* in Peredelkino, a beautiful village near Moscow, belonged to Boris Pasternak, the poet.
Important Party and government officials are given even more grander establishments in the countryside
around big cities and in resort areas like the Crimea.

exceptions) have never traveled in a way that would have allowed them to absorb the atmosphere or way of life in another land.

An important change has occurred in the attitude of Soviet leaders since the death of Stalin. He ruled with fear. Stalin's subordinates did his bidding or faced the possibility of the direst consequences. Fear has been taken out of the equation, and today's rulers govern with blandishments and bribes instead. In recent years the system of privileges for important people has both grown enormously and been systematized, so that ambitious Soviet citizens can know with some precision what material benefits will accompany each promotion in their careers. The modern Soviet leadership has given an ever-broader section of the population a share of the benefits of power. The recipients of this largess develop a loyalty to the leaders and to the status quo that is probably more reliable than the loyalty Stalin exacted through terror.

Lesser figures receive lesser *Dachas*, like these along a highway northeast of Moscow.

The state maintains vast networks of special facilities for the privileged, from special shops and services to special holiday resorts, apartment houses, and even an entire national network of clinics and hospitals. These health facilities are run by a separate national bureaucracy, the Fourth Department of the Ministry of Health. The Fourth Department actually publishes a book for its clinics outlining precisely what sort of treatment—in what sort of room, with what sort of furnishings and equipment—each level of the state and Communist party bureaucracy is entitled to receive.

The material benefits of life at the top have created widespread greed and cynicism. Andrei Sakharov, the famous dissident physicist, tells a revealing story about the time he asked a colleague, Prof. Alexander Imshyenetsky, to help find a job for a young scientist who had gotten into hot water with the authorities. Prof. Imshyenetsky declined to help, saying: "I am not going to make any trouble for Soviet power. It has allowed me to go abroad thirty-six times."

134

This building is unmarked, but many Muscovites know it as the Kremlin Polyclinic, where the country's most important men go for medical care. The long black car in front is a ZIL limousine, a custom-made automobile of which perhaps a dozen are produced each year. Only members of the politburo use the ZIL limousines.

Klose

"Soviet power" means the powers that be, and Prof. Imshyenetsky was reminding Sakharov that he was one of their favored few. His reference to trips abroad is not surprising; foreign travel is perhaps the greatest privilege Soviet power can bestow. A trip to the West brings instant status—and allows the traveler to buy the record albums and blue jeans that are so avidly sought by Russians, and particularly by younger members of the privileged class.

Poliakov

Abdalov

Pravda, the official organ of the Communist party, is posted on city bulletin boards like this one so passing citizens can catch up with the news. In fact, there is very little news in *Pravda,* and a great deal of exhortation and propaganda. The man reading the paper here is a typical member of the intelligentsia, or educated class. His shoes, briefcase, gloves, overcoat, scarf, and hat are all badges of high status in Soviet society.

This sign on a building in an old quarter of central Moscow marks the headquarters of the "Main Directorate for the Protection of State Secrets in the Press, Under the Council of Ministers of the USSR." No printed material of any kind—not even a theater program—can be circulated in the Soviet Union without being read and approved by the censor.

The gulf between leaders and led is the subject of many Soviet jokes. A typical one concerns Brezhnev and his elderly mother. According to the story, she left her country village at her son's urging to visit him at his hunting lodge on the Volga. Brezhnev showed the simple peasant woman around the grand house, pointing to the wood paneling, the silverware, the sunken bath and swimming pool. "Well, mama," Brezhnev said at the end of the tour, "how do you like it?"

A political lecturer and his audience. The lecturer is expected to give his listeners a livelier and more informative account of some current event or situation than can be found in the Soviet press. The audience here consists of policemen, employees of the Ministry of Internal Affairs.

"Oh, Leonid," she replied, "it's marvelous. But aren't you afraid the Bolsheviks might come back?"

The leaders' high standard of living may contradict the egalitarian rhetoric of Marxism-Leninism, but this is a contradiction that Soviet citizens appear to take for granted. Indeed, Soviet citizens learn from an early age to tolerate a great deal of official hokum. The official Soviet version of reality has been altered so often just during the last generation that anyone paying even vague attention has perceived the inconsistencies.

The regime's information policies encourage public cynicism. Besides altering important historical information—for example, transforming Stalin from the father of the nation to a malefactor to a nonperson to, most recently, a revered wartime leader—the authorities stick doggedly to good news, usually ignoring all else; so citizens only learn of airplane crashes if a friend or relative dies in one. The news media almost never report accidents. The shops may be bare, but the papers constantly report on the triumphs of the Five Year Plan.

Uzlyan   Abdalov

A civil defense lecture at the Moscow
Institute of Cinematography. The
Lecturer is speaking before a bulletin
board that describes nuclear explosions
and the preparations that can be made
to protect against them. The mask is
what people will be wearing after an
attack.

Here the lecture is historical—a
reading from a biography of Lenin. The
audience consists of the managerial
employees of a big collective farm.
Their intent expressions suggest that
they were paying attention to the
photographer from a Moscow
newspaper as well as to the lecturer.

Soviet society buzzes with rumors, no doubt a result of popular mistrust of the official news media. A Russian woman who worked as a cook for a British diplomat in Moscow once asked her employer what had happened to Vladimir Komarov, a Soviet cosmonaut. That very day Komarov had been given a hero's burial in the Kremlin wall after a space accident—as the Russian woman's employer told her.

"Oh, it's really true then?" the cook replied. "We'd heard that he had brought his spaceship down in America and defected."

The authorities recognize the inadequacy of their news media as actual conveyors of news. They compensate partially by sending official lecturers around the country to speak on political subjects at schools, factories, and Party meetings. Lecturers talk more freely than writers for *Pravda* can write, and they often cite facts and figures that aren't printed openly. But in the provinces, lecturers are notoriously dull, and the regular political lecture is an ordeal to be endured.

Important officials, including editors of the official newspapers, receive special news bulletins that contain uncensored information and reports from abroad that are never published in the open press. Citizens from all ranks and conditions now listen to Russian language broadcasts from foreign radio stations, particularly the Voice of America, the British Broadcasting Corporation, and West German Radio. These stations provide an alternative version of reality that seems to please the Soviet audience.

Widespread public skepticism should not be confused with outright opposition, however. Most citizens seem to allow their skepticism to coexist with essential loyalty to the Soviet system and even faith in its basic tenets. Soviet citizens organize their lives and ambitions around the possibilities that the system offers. They do not think or talk much of changing the system.

Russians have been going along with their leaders for many centuries. Their willingness to submit to the power of the day provoked Alexander Pushkin early in the last century to write these angry verses about his countrymen:

> *Graze on, ye peaceful sheep and cattle,*
> *The call of honor cannot grip*
> *Or charm you into freedom's battle. . . .*

Gluck

This is the scene at a soccer football game—soldiers at intervals of about a yard ring the entire stadium like this, ready to quell any spontaneous manifestation by the crowd. Control is a constant preoccupation of the Soviet authorities—control of the anarchic instincts within themselves that most Russians seem to fear.

Jews trying to emigrate to Israel were one of many dissident groups who began to challenge the authorities with unprecedented boldness during the 1970s. Here a group of "refuseniks," Jews whose applications for exit visas had been refused, demonstrate outside the Ministry of Internal Affairs in Moscow. Their signs read, "Let Us Go to Israel," "Visas to Israel instead of jail," or simply, "I Want to Go to Israel." The man on the right in the hat and dark raincoat is a policeman who has just begun to rip up the demonstrators' signs.

Joseloff

Kaliningrad (formerly Königsberg). World War II is a constant presence in contemporary Soviet life. Russians call it "the Great Patriotic War"; reminders of it and memorials to it are everywhere. The authorities keep alive the memory with unceasing propaganda, plays, films, and books. The war legitimized the Bolshevik revolution, because it gave the Bolsheviks their chance to save Russia, which they did.

The Soviet Union lost 20 million people in the war, and countless more were maimed.

WAR

Kaspiev

Abdalov

War veterans' reunions. The two moods suggest the country's ambivalent memories of the war—partly happy, because that was a time of common sacrifice and achievement, partly tragic.

In every town and city there is a war memorial, often with an eternal flame, often guarded in shifts by Young Pioneers in uniform, like this one. These are residents of Stalingrad, now known as Volgograd, whose city was destroyed in the War and has now been completely rebuilt.

ndrei Amalrik, one of the best-known of the recent generation of dissident Soviet intellectuals, lived in exile in a remote Siberian village in the mid-1960s, an experience he later described in a book. "I think that these are people with whom you can do anything," he wrote in despair of the peasants in his village. In another book, Amalrik reflected on the Russian view of personal freedom:

"The very word 'freedom' is understood by most people as a synonym of the word 'disorders,' as an opportunity of executing with impunity some kind of antisocial or dangerous action. . . ."

But if most Russians will always go along, a few always won't. This seems to be inevitable in a system built on myths. A few people who learn to think for themselves, who develop strong values and respect for the truth, are destined eventually to think out loud.

In our time, the rebellious intellectuals have become famous as "dissidents," a brave if tiny band of independent souls whose activities have come to the attention of the entire world. Indeed, Alexander Solzhenitsyn and Andrei Sakharov are both better known outside the Soviet Union than the men who belong to the ruling Soviet politburo.

This latest phase of the historic struggle between Russian state authority and free-thinking Russian intellectuals began with the post-Stalin "thaw" in the late 1950s. The end of Stalin's terrorism and the sudden change in the Party line enunciated by Nikita Khrushchev gave the country's writers and intellectuals an entirely new sense of their own prospects. Writers published works that would have been unthinkable a few years earlier. Foreigners began to be allowed into the country. Ideas began to percolate. It was heady stuff for the intelligentsia, but a little too scary for the leadership. Khrushchev himself began ot tighten the screws in the early 1960s, and the men who threw him out of power in 1964 continued that process purposefully.

It was this crackdown in the late 1960s that produced the dissidents. They first appeared in 1966 in open protests against the trial of two Russian writers, Andrei Sinyavski and Yuli Daniel, who were prosecuted for using pseudonyms to publish books in the West that displeased the Soviet authorities. It was the first time Soviet writers had been sent to prison for what they had written, an ominous turn that formally marked the end of the thaw and the beginning of the modern dissident movement. Movement may be a misleading word. The dissidents are an extraordinarily diverse group. The most famous ones are Moscow intellectuals, but they often disagree among themselves. There are also Russian nationalist dissidents who disapprove of both communism and the multinational Soviet

Abdalov

Artists can be dissidents too. In the 1970s many painters whose work was too "subjective"—that is, insufficiently realistic—to suit the authorities began to seek ways to show their works. One large exhibit in a field outside Moscow was broken up by police and a water truck, but this one was permitted to go on unmolested.

Andrei D. Sakharov, inventor of the Soviet hydrogen bomb, winner of the Nobel prize for peace, "a crystal of morality," as Nikita Khrushchev once called him. Here Sakharov gives a press conference in his Moscow apartment for reporters from western news media. When Sakharov lived in Moscow, the political police, the KGB, took over the flat upstairs so they could listen in on events like this one.

Wide World Photos

state; religious dissidents who refuse to accept state restrictions on religious practice; and many different kinds of nationalist dissidents in the non-Russian Soviet republics.

The modern dissidents are unique in one significant respect. They have attracted an international audience, bringing foreigners into an internal Russian debate. By the early 1970s, frustrated intellectuals in Moscow were meeting regularly with western correspondents, passing on news of dissident activities or harassment by the political police, the KGB. In 1973, Andrei Sakharov began holding regular press conferences in his Moscow flat to pass on the latest news.

Western journalists not only brought news of the dissidents to the outside world; they also informed the Soviet public. The western radio stations broadcasting in Russian pick up the news reported from Moscow and send it back into the USSR. The channels established between unhappy Soviet citizens and western reporters became a link between a sort of domestic opposition—albeit weak and disorganized—and the Soviet masses.

This has been an alarming turn of events for the Soviet leaders, and they have done their best to restore orthodoxy and normalcy. The official campaign to silence the dissidents that began in the 1960s

A juvenile prison. The banner at the far end of the hall is a conventional propaganda slogan: "Art, like literature, is a powerful tool in the communist upbringing of the Soviet people."

continued throughout the 1970s, and it was largely successful. Those who signed protests were punished; those who organized them were sent to labor camps, prisons, or psychiatric hospitals. Thousands of unhappy intellectuals chose to leave the country by joining the Jewish emigration movement—whether or not they were actually Jewish.

Once engaged in a serious struggle with the dissidents, the authorities were bound to prevail. With their vast political police force and totalitarian control over every citizen's daily life, from school or university to job and home, the authorities hold all the cards. During the 1970s, when detente with the West seemed important to the Soviet leaders, they allowed some dissidence to continue, apparently because they would not pay the price for stamping it out. But after the invasion of Afghanistan and the worsening of East-West relations that followed, the authorities no longer felt restrained. Their decision to arrest and expel from Moscow Andrei Sakharov symbolized perhaps the final phase of the latest dissident movement.

But if the latest episode in the ancient struggle between Russian autocrats and Russian intellectuals has ended, the struggle will continue. New dissidents will appear, new protests will be made, because that is in the nature of the system.

Poliakov

Aid to the Russian Church

A KGB prison in Leningrad, its windows covered so that
no one can see in or out.

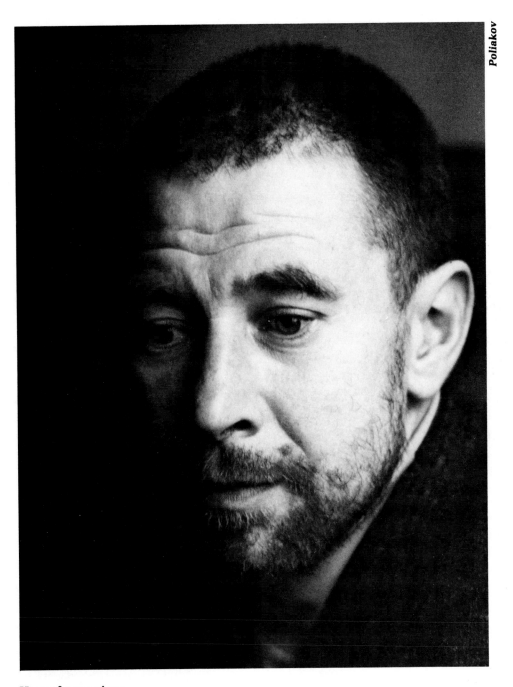

Poliakov

Home from prison.

This is the special psychiatric hospital at Oryol, one of the psychiatric
institutions used for the forced treatment of political dissidents. This was a
widespread practice in the 1960s and early 1970s, but pressure from abroad,
particularly from the international psychiatric community, has apparently
convinced the Soviet authorities to use this sort of "treatment" much less often.

A TRIAL

This series of photographs was taken during a trial held in Podolski, a small town near Moscow. The defendant, a young man named Nikolai, was charged with "political hooliganism" after fellow workers in his factory identified him as the man responsible for decorating the plant with graffiti.

The graffiti carried angry messages: Why is there no meat in the stores? Where are our human rights? Why is our pay so low? Why are our elections rigged? Nikolai used a special, difficult-to-remove paint, provided by a friend, to put these messages on walls all around the factory. The woman who looked after the factory washrooms testified that she found fresh graffiti on the men's room wall right after seeing Nikolai leave.

Alexander Uzlian, the photographer who took these unique pictures, recalls that prosecution and defense both sought to portray Nikolai as a drunkard who didn't really know what he was doing. This explanation suited the prosecution, because it removed any need to explain why a Soviet citizen would criticize the state. It appealed also to the defense as the best way to minimize the punishment that the three-member "peoples' court" would decree. As in virtually all such cases, conviction was a foregone conclusion once the matter was brought to trial.

Testifying on his own behalf, Nikolai told the court that he was drunk when he painted the graffiti, he couldn't explain why he did it. His father was killed at the front during the Great Patriotic War (World War II), he noted, hoping this might be mitigating evidence. Uzlian thought many in the audience were privately sympathetic to Nikolai, but the court sentenced him to seven years exile in a remote corner of Siberia.

Uzlyan

The Peoples' Court in Podolski, near Moscow. Nikolai sits before his three judges.

The washroom attendant who found freshly painted graffiti just after Nikolai left the men's room.

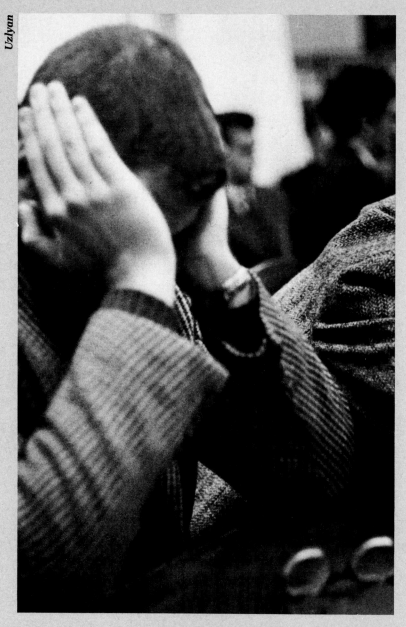

Uzlyan

Nikolai's comrade who gave him the paint
he used for the graffiti.

Nikolai's mother, daughter,
and wife watch the trial.

Uzlyan   Uzlyan

Uzlyan

The public was invited.

Nikolai's wife has just seen him off on the train that will take him to the remote Siberian village where he will spend his seven-year term of exile.

Uzlyan

AT WORK

The Soviet Union is the world's second superpower. According to all the published statistics, it is an economic giant, second only to the United States. Nevertheless, if a citizen of Moscow (let alone a lesser provincial town) wanted to buy a carpet for his apartment, he could search the city's stores in vain trying to find one.

The world's second superpower is increasingly a participant in world commerce, trading more every year with the capitalist world. But the balance sheet of Soviet trade reads like that of an underdeveloped country: purchases of advanced machinery and consumer goods, sales of raw materials and precious metals.

The Soviet Union leads the world in the production of steel, but it has barely entered the computer era. The developed capitalist countries have passed through three generations of computerization and now rely on computers in every phase of their economic life. The Soviet Union has missed all three generations, and uses computers only in a few specialized areas. When the Soviets try seriously to catch up to modern methods of data processing and transmission, they will find that their national telephone system is far too primitive to cope.

The anomalies and absurdities of the Soviet economy could fill a long book. No doubt this contradictory record is a source of deep frustration for the Soviet leadership. Yes, the Stalinist economic machine has modernized a backward country, produced a splendid military machine, made the Soviet Union a power to be dealt with all over the world. Yes, too, alas, the country remains backward in many respects, and is utterly unable to compete with the capitalist countries as an industrial, financial, or technological power.

The strength and the weakness of the Soviet economic system is the Plan. By exploiting the ability centrally to plan the entire economy, the Soviet leaders can concentrate the country's resources on a narrow range of goals they deem most important. But by eliminating traditional economic incentives and artificially controlling the development process, the Plan assures a lack of innovation, shoddy workmanship, and a host of other problems.

The accomplishments wrought by the Plan can be staggering. The most impressive may be the giant "hero projects" that are the centerpiece of each Five-Year Plan. The present one is the Baikal-Amur Magistral, or BAM, a new railroad that is being built across a remote and godforsaken stretch of eastern Siberia, hundreds of miles to the north of the original Trans-Siberian. BAM will cost billions of rubles and involve the labor of tens of thousands of Soviet workers, many of them young people

A new bridge spans the Volga near the town of Engels. Huge girders like these help explain why the Soviet Union is now the world's largest producer of steel.

Steel workers work with molten metal at a vast metallurgical complex in the industrial center of Chelyabinsk.

A Soviet rocket rushes through Red Square in the November 7 parade.

Young workers lay track for the Baikal-Amur Magistral (BAM), the hero project of the latest Five-Year Plan. The government has induced thousands of young people to work on this project, a remote but important new rail link between populated areas and the rich natural resources of northeastern Siberia.

The assembly line at Togliattigrad, where the Soviets constructed an automobile factory that makes virtually every part of the car, then assembles it. The factory, a hero project in the twenty-third five-year plan, was purchased from Italy.

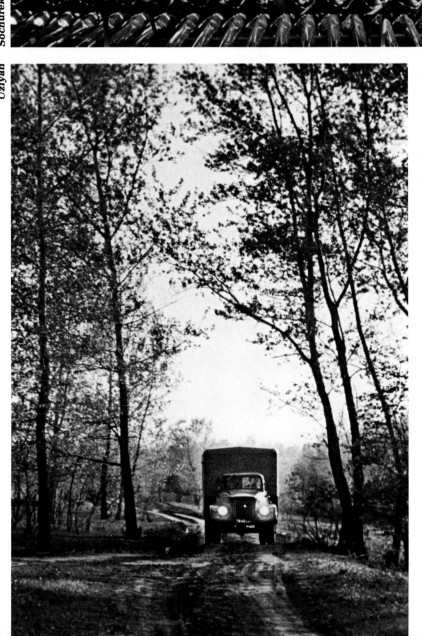

Dirt roads are still common all over the country. Altogether the Soviet Union has less than 300,000 miles of paved roads. The United States, with half as much territory, has 4 million miles.

A young cellist in recital. The Russians train musicians just the way they build modern intercontinental ballistic missiles—by lavishing resources on a narrow and precise objective.

drawn to the project by the prospect of adventure, unusually high pay, and the prestige of working on a hero project. BAM is being built on permafrost, the permanent layer of ice that lies under a thin crust of earth in most of Northern Siberia, an area rich in oil and minerals that are extremely difficult to extract. Most work in this area must be completed in the brief, hot, mosquito-ridden summer. For eight or nine months a year Siberia is frozen solid.

The hero project in the previous Five-Year Plan was a mammoth truck factory built in a prairie on the Kama River near the Urals. That factory was modeled on the hero project which preceded it—the giant Fiat factory bought from Italy and built at Togliattigrad. Both of these projects were intended to compensate with one grand stroke the basic inadequacies in the Soviet economy—shortages of cars and trucks.

The scale of these projects is not easy to imagine. Rarely if ever do capitalists attempt such efforts. The Fiat factory, for example, could not depend on any external source for parts; so it had to manufacture virtually every item necessary to make an automobile, from the plastic knobs on the dashboard to the seatcovers, sparkplugs, and shock absorbers. (Only electrical equipment, glass, and tires came from other plants.) One of the biggest parts of the KAMAz project was the foundry built on the site to make all the steel the plant would need. In both these cases the factories were built in uninhabited spots, so entire cities had to be build around them too.

These projects invariably cost more than they were supposed to and are completed years behind schedule, but the more important fact surely is their ultimate success. It is not surprising that the state undertakes just one of these monsters every five years. It could not find the resources for more.

The same kind of lavish expenditure of resources and effort explains nearly every Soviet success, from intercontinental ballistic missiles to ballet dancers and pianists. There is no secret explanation for the Soviets' ability to all but match American military technology; they do it by exerting a staggering effort, greater probably than even the most alarming measurements of Soviet "defense spending"suggest. It is unlikely that missile factories—or ballet schools—are inherently more efficient than, say, the notorious Ministry of Agriculture. They produce better results because of the resources they receive and because of their status within the country, which helps the favored enterprises attract the best people.

Missile factories are closed to outsiders, but it is possible to visit the Central Music School in Moscow, which is probably a typical privileged institution. Like rockets, music is one of the Soviet Union's top priorities. Soviet musicians bring honor and prestige to the motherland while maintaining a rich Russian musical tradition.

The Central Music School in Moscow is one of 5,000 Soviet schools that offer children aged seven to seventeen special music training, and one of thirty extraordinary schools for the most gifted children. Each of the thirty is attached to a college-level conservatory. At the Moscow school there are 100 teachers for 350 students, a ratio that ensures intense, individualized instruction. The best students are encouraged to practice their instruments six hours a day. They begin giving concerts at age seven or eight, and by seventeen the most talented are accomplished professional musicians.

Such methods are effective without being efficient. Indeed, they are very expensive. The degree to which resources are lavished on hero projects, pianists, and missiles is also a measure of how impoverished other sectors of the society must remain.

This is the explanation for the paradoxical nature of Soviet economic development. It is largely because of the efforts made to produce missiles and ballet dancers that many of the Soviet citizens who live in rural areas (about a third of the population) are not served by electricity, or have no indoor plumbing. There may be no carpets for sale because the State Planning Commission puts no emphasis on carpets. Rural poverty and woefully inadequate consumer goods are among the costs of doing well in priority areas.

Admiring the production at the plate-glass factory in Gorki. Soviet factories do not try to make profits, they try to fulfill the "Plan," a set of goals established for each factory by government authorities. Soviet plate glass is notoriously thin and brittle, because factory directors have found they can more easily fulfill the Plan by making the glass thin, thus stretching the same amount of raw materials over a larger area.

According to the Plan, this mountain of potatoes should have been transported to a proper storage facility, but instead they have been left here to rot. Transportation bottlenecks are endemic in the Soviet economy, and cause great waste. Here two resourceful citizens make an effort at to least reduce the number of potatoes that will be ruined.

Kaiser   Uzlyan

Uneven development is only one of the weaknesses of the Soviet planned economy. In the name of the Plan, the Soviets put up with all kinds of inefficiency, waste, and confusion. Perhaps most important of all, the Plan becomes a deterrent to innovation or experimentation by individual enterprises.

The enormity of the task of planning the Soviet economy is not easily grasped. Take the industrial sector, for example. There is no free market in any raw material; every factory is allocated the materials (and, to a large extent, the labor) that the central planners think it will need. Nor can an enterprise look for its own customers—the central planners also allocate finished products to users.

This picture was taken at midmorning on a weekday, but there wasn't a worker in sight. To fulfill the Plan, construction enterprises routinely begin more work than they can finish; then spread the available workforce thinly among the unfinished projects. Unfinished apartment houses like this one are a common sight in the Soviet Union.

Kaiser

Heros of labor leave their coal mine with bouquets of flowers, bestowed on them
for successfully fulfilling the Plan.

Workers' motorcycles parked in front of the "Board of Honor" outside a Soviet factory. The men whose
pictures are on display are "Cavaliers of the Order of Lenin," whose outstanding work has been
rewarded with that prize.

The State Planning Commission, working with government ministries that oversee various branches of industry, takes responsibility for balancing the inputs and outputs of the entire, enormous Soviet industrial network. One mistake in a vital area can be disastrous. For example, a 10 percent shortfall in the production of concrete could throw off the construction plan for the entire nation, leaving factories without the new buildings they were counting on to meet their plans, leaving roads unbuilt that were crucial to the fulfillment of yet other plans, and so forth.

In fact, the Soviets have discovered that it is just too difficult to plan every aspect of a complex industrial economy. So, they concentrate on output, leaving much else to fate. Distribution is a good example of a neglected sector; the economy is hobbled by bottlenecks caused by inadequate supplies of trucks, paved roads, warehouses, and so on. Losses "in transit" are endemic. A Soviet newspaper once reported that 30 percent of the trees harvested in Soviet forests are lost or ruined before they can be turned into lumber or pulp.

Even the term "output" is ambiguous in a planned economy. How should it be measured? In the capitalist world, output is measured in terms of its value in the marketplace, but in the Soviet Union there is no marketplace, and items have no inherent value. Even the ruble has no fixed value, since all prices are set arbitrarily by the planners, not the market. So the planners must establish targets for output based on measurements other than value.

This creates all sorts of absurdities. A classic one involves the production of plate glass. What is the proper way to measure the output of a plate-glass factory? Should the measure be purely quantitative, or should the quality of the product make a difference? If quantity is all that matters, how should it be measured? The Soviets have decided to measure the output of plate glass in terms of square meters of glass produced.

Once the Plan is established, a factory director and everyone who works for him knows what must be done to satisfy their superiors, and to earn bonuses that can range from an extra month's salary to as much as an additional 30 percent in pay: They must fulfill or overfulfill the Plan targets for square meters of glass.

For the director of a plate-glass factory, maximizing the output of square meters of glass involves a relatively simple computation. He is supplied with a fixed amount of raw materials—sand, potash, and so on—and a known technological process. Expanding production isn't easy, unless perhaps the glass can be made *thinner*, thus spreading the same amount of raw materials over a greater number

At the Neurosurgical Institute in Moscow, every piece of equipment in the operating room is foreign-made.

of square meters. This is indeed the option plate-glass factories choose. Soviet window glass is notoriously thin and fragile. Windows installed in prefabricated building panels are routinely shattered before they can be installed at a building site.

The planning system produces countless absurdities of this kind. A Soviet newspaper once discovered, for example, that a factory making men's suits had become famous for producing suits that shrank. The paper sent a reporter to investigate. It turned out that the factory knew its suits would shrink, but blamed the problem on its supplier of textiles for failing to provide preshrunk fabric. The reporter asked why the clothing factory didn't do the preshrinking. The answer was simple: If the factory accepted delivery of 100,000 meters of cloth then preshrunk away 10 percent of it, fulfillment of the Plan would be impossible.

The Plan also distorts the pace of work in Soviet enterprises. Typically the annual Plan is divided into monthly and quarterly targets that are also supposed to be met on time. These deadlines have produced a phenomenon that Soviet economists have named "storming," the exertion of enormous effort in the closing days of each month or quarter to meet Plan's deadlines. Factory executives routinely live at their plants during the last four or five days of the month to oversee the storm. In one Soviet republic, a senior official revealed, the average factory produced half of its monthly output in

A professor of mathematics at the "Academic City" in Novosibirsk explains a theory. Soviet theoretical mathematicians are among the best in the world.

Assembling a new computer. The Soviets have not been able to master the mass production of computers, which are still largely handmade. The Soviet economy has missed the computer revolution that transformed the capitalist world, and the effective use of computers is still unusual in Soviet industry.

Working with a particle accelerator in a nuclear physics laboratory. Advanced nuclear physics is another field in which Soviet scientists have excelled.

the last ten days of the month. This cannot be an efficient method of production, but then, the Russian language does not have a word for efficiency.

Despite the formal appearance of the Plan, a factory director in the USSR knows that nothing is certain. The authorities can raise his targets at any time, but they cannot guarantee the delivery of his materials, since they must be produced by other enterprises that may not be able to meet their own production targets. A clever industrial administrator is constantly wooing his superiors to hold his targets as low as possible, and wooing suppliers to be sure he gets the materials he needs. This is the situation that so discourages innovation and technological experimentation.

A factory director who has established good working relations with his suppliers and his superiors and who has the combination of equipment and labor that he needs to meet his Plan targets has no interest whatsoever in making "progress"—or in making any changes.

Prof. Gersh Budker and a student work in Budker's Institute of Nuclear Physics in Novosibirsk. Budker is one of the Soviet Union's most resourceful and gifted scientists. But his laboratory suffers from a chronic shortage of the necessary equipment to conduct advanced experiments.

Innovation would probably require new raw materials, new skills in the work force, and a reorganization of the factory's production line. Innovation would certainly lead to new, higher production targets, since that is the point of innovating. This might mean progress to some bureaucrat in Moscow, but to the men running the factory it means trouble—trouble finding and befriending new suppliers and workers, trouble learning to run and maintain new machinery, trouble satisfying new, higher targets.

The essence of the Soviet system is central control; so eventually innovations can be imposed even on reluctant enterprises. But imposed innovation is bound to be less successful than a more spontaneous change, and the most effective innovations are probably those that might be developed inside a factory, not in a Moscow ministry. But the Soviet resists all forms of spontaneity.

The Soviet economy's instinctive resistance to innovation largely explains why the second superpower remains technologically backward by comparison with the capitalist countries. In competitive conditions an important technological improvement is sucked into use like air into a vacuum—the competitors must make the innovation or lose the competition. That is how the capitalist world was computerized in a generation—once someone started using computers, others had to follow quickly or face an insurmountable competitive disadvantage. There is no comparable force at work in the Soviet Union.

Relative Soviet backwardness is also a function of erratic development of Soviet science. *Sputnik* mobilized America by raising the fear that Soviet science had become the world's best, but it is now clear that this was far from the case. Despite huge expenditures on the training of vast quantities of scientists, the Soviets remain far behind the international vanguard in most fields of scientific research.

The theoretical work by Russian scientists, significantly, is excellent. Soviet mathematics, for example, is as good as any in the world. But when it comes to transforming theory into practice, the Soviets begin to have trouble. Thanks to expanded scientific exchanges during the 1970s, foreigners, particularly Americans, have had unprecedented access to the Soviet scientific establishment. What they have found is inefficiency, rigidity, poor equipment, and a lack of independence from the whims of political authorities—a combination that prevents the Soviet Union from fulfilling its own ambitions to become a scientific power.

The story of Gersh Budker is a good example. Budker is a brilliant nuclear physicist who established the Institute of Nuclear Physics at Novosibirsk in 1958. The institute was part of "Academgorodok," a new academic center promoted by Nikita Khrushchev, partly as a way to give younger scientists a chance to show what they could do in new research institutes of their own.

Budker assembled a staff of bright young people and soon began to produce research work that put his institute in the forefront of nuclear physics in the world. But according to a young physicist who worked there for many years, Budker could not sustain his accomplishments. The whole laboratory knew that once an important new discovery of theirs was described in an academic journal, foreigners would master it and probably surpass it in a short period of time. "This doesn't depend on how smart you are," the physicist who worked with Budker explained. "It's because of the low level of our technology."

A Soviet factory. Women share manufacturing jobs on an equal footing with men.

Morning exercises at the textile factory in Ivanova, where the workforce is entirely female.

Soldiers are often pressed into civilian construction work. These five enlisted men have been laying bricks with an attention to neatness and detail that typifies Soviet workmanship.

Budker has always suffered from insufficient scientific equipment. To compensate he created his own little workshop to make sophisticated instruments. The workshop was so successful that it eventually provided half the institute's budget by selling instruments to other laboratories. But do-it-yourself instrumentation is no way to keep pace with the well-financed and equipped researchers in the West, so Budker is always trying to think of areas into which his group can plunge so they can stay on the front line of world physics. American scientists now know, as one of them has put it, that "when the Soviets make a very important discovery, it is extremely likely that we will get more benefit out of it than they do."

Because of strict political controls on foreign travel, Soviet scientists are only erratic participants in the international scientific community. Often the brightest young people are denied permission to attend meetings in other countries, while trusted but undistinguished senior colleagues are sent in their place. Only rarely can a gifted Soviet scientist get permission to spend an extended period in a foreign laboratory, though such exchanges are common for other nations' researchers. Young people

These women are bus conductors, taking time out for breakfast. Passengers in the bus behind are waiting for them to finish.

Lunch in the factory dining room.

are also forced to wait, often for many years, to get important posts inside the rigidly structured Soviet scientific hierarchy.

Perhaps the best symbol of Soviet science is the very space program that first alerted the outside world that something was going on in the USSR. For years it was assumed all over the world that the Soviets led in the "space race." But by the time America's moon program—conceived as a riposte to the USSR—got seriously underway, the Soviets had actually dropped out of the contest. We now know that they were never in the race to the moon; they could not master the rocket engine technology, miniaturization, metallurgy, and electronics that made the Apollo missions work. Their early successes, we now know, were the products of brilliant improvisation. For example, they could never make large rocket engines; so they simply added more and more engines to the same rocket. The *Vostok* that took Yuri Gagarin into space was propelled by twenty separate engines all clustered together.

Of course, Gagarin did get into space. The Russians are far from feeble; their problem is that they cannot do as well as they would like. In science as in other fields, they often turn abroad for help. Nothing is so prized in a Soviet laboratory as a piece of foreign equipment. Soviet scientists who have met foreign colleagues often write them asking for gifts of small items.

Why can't Russians make good scientific equipment? It is a baffling question, one they ask themselves all the time. Part of the answer, surely, is endemic sloppiness. Soviet workers are notorious for their cavalier attitude toward quality control.

In fact, judging by what the Russians write in their own newspapers, poor performance by workers is a chronic problem in the "workers' state." The papers constantly rail about drunkenness on the job, malingering, absenteeism, and the stealing of "socialist property" from places of employment. Foreign engineers and businessmen who have worked in Soviet plants (generally after their firms had sold some equipment to the USSR) report a widespread lack of discipline and workmanship. They also note that Soviet workers often have a very narrow sense of their own role, and display no interest in improvising on the job.

This sort of narrow rigidity seems typical of the system. In Israel, Soviet émigré engineers have found that they were trained for so narrow a specialty that a small country like Israel can't really use their skills. Soviet workers spend months or years being taught the most basic skills. The army, for instance, spends a year teaching recruits how to drive a car. Russians seem to have special schools for nearly everything—waiters, for example, or tractor drivers.

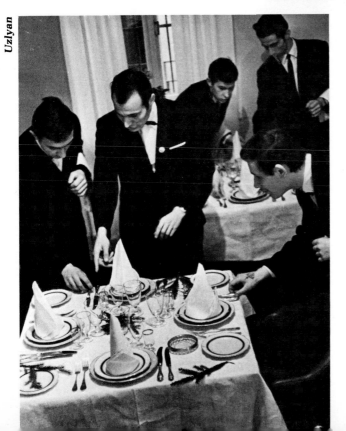

Russians seem to have schools for nearly every imaginable profession. These are institutes for the training of waiters, chefs, and clowns.

In the far north of Siberia, where much of the Soviet Union's natural wealth is buried, new buildings must be constructed in permafrost, the layer of ice that lies just below the surface. These piles, sunk deep into that ice, will support a new structure, but it may be summer before work on it can begin.

But the most serious problem with the work force is strictly quantitative; it is ceasing to grow. By the 1990s, the Soviets reckon, they will have to learn to live with a constant work force—no growth at all. For many years they have depended on a constantly growing pool of workers. First peasants were drawn to the cities, then women were drawn into the work force, then industry was brought to the outlying areas with population surpluses. Now all the gimmicks have been exhausted. Soviet planners hope to increase labor productivity (it is now about half that in the United States), but this will not be easy.

Permafrost heaves and sinks with the seasons, making the construction of ordinary roads extremely difficult. Here residents of Yakutia in far northeastern Siberia build a road from sections of logs that will rise up and down independently, thus preserving the essential roadway even if it gets quite bumpy.

Declining growth of the population is just one of the fundamental economic problems that will bedevil the Soviet Union in the years to come. Another is the Soviets' persistent inability to modernize and innovate. A third is the increasing difficulty of exploiting the country's vast natural resources.

Until now the steady growth of Soviet industry has depended on a combination of abundant resources and abundant labor. The resources remain abundant; no country in the world can match the Soviets' reserves of oil, gas, minerals, and timber, or their capacity for generating hydroelectric power. But the easily exploited resources are nearly exhausted; what remains is remote from European Russia and often difficult to get at. The next generation will have to learn how to retrieve natural riches that are beyond the reach of present Soviet capabilities.

In every category of importance, today's Soviet capabilities seem insufficient to meet tomorrow's challenges. The USSR must develop stronger and better-educated leadership; it must resolve festering tensions among the country's many national groups; it must compensate for a faltering birth rate; and revive a stumbling economy. Some of the best minds in the Soviet Union long ago came to the conclusion that radical reforms are necessary to sustain the Soviet status as a superpower into the next century. But radical reform scares Russians, and it terrifies Communist bureaucrats. There have been no radical reforms in Russia since Stalin's time.

The Soviets have great advantages to exploit—their country's natural wealth, the patriotism and patience of their citizens, and a great national history that has always provided inspiration for a better future. But the way ahead is neither clear nor direct, and a lot can go wrong.

The Baikal-Amur Magistral is the Soviet Union's latest Hero Project, an endeavor that involves hundreds of millions of rubles and tens of thousands of workers. But the level of effort apparently cannot overcome the fact that the tracks must be laid on unstable permafrost in northeastern Siberia. The result is a railroad line that suggests a metaphor for the future of Soviet Russia.

Sochurek

ALEXANDER UZLYAN was born in Rostov-on-Don in 1908. He graduated from the Soviet Higher State Institute of Cinematography, and began his career in photojournalism in the 1930s on the staff of *Komsomolskaya Pravda*, the newspaper of the Young Communist League. Uzlyan soon became one of the Soviet Union's best-known photographers. He worked for numerous newspapers and magazines, and his photographs received numerous prizes and honors. His wartime photographs, taken on many fronts during World War II, made Uzlyan famous. Some of those pictures appeared in *The Russian War: 1941–45*, published by E. P. Dutton in 1978. Uzlyan's work first appeared in America in 1955, in the New York Museum of Modern Art's famous "Family of Man" exhibition. Uzlyan emigrated from the Soviet Union in 1975 and now lives in Silver Spring, Maryland, with his wife and daughter.

HOWARD SOCHUREK is an American photographer who has been in the Soviet Union on twenty-four different visits. In 1958 he opened the *Life* magazine bureau in Moscow, and stayed there for two years. For many years he was one of *Life*'s best-known contributors, and since the magazine ceased weekly publication he has been a successful freelance photographer. Sochurek's photographs have appeared often in the *National Geographic, Fortune, Time,* and the *Smithsonian* magazine. He is married to a woman of Russian origin and has studied the Soviet Union at Harvard as a Nieman Fellow. Sochurek lives with his wife and daughter in Scarsdale, New York.

VICTOR ABDALOV is a young filmmaker who was born in Ashkhabad, Soviet Turkmenia, in 1949. He grew up in Turkmenia, then studied at the All-Union Institute of Cinematography in Moscow. He made several short films in the Soviet Union, and also began actively taking photographs. In 1975 he emigrated from the Soviet Union, and in the years since he has undertaken a number of photographic projects. A show of his pictures was given in conjunction with the International Sakharov Hearings in Washington in 1979. Abdalov now lives in Washington with his American-born wife.

LEV POLIAKOV, born in Leningrad in 1934, has taught skiing, worked as an underwater film cameraman, made films of heart surgeons at work, and taught film in a varied career in his homeland before immigrating to America in 1973. In this country, he has taken underwater photographs for the Cousteau Society, served as the staff photographer of a New York hospital, and worked on freelance assignments for several publications. Poliakov lives in New York.

YURI SHALAMOV was one of the Soviet Union's best-known sports photographers before he immigrated to America in 1974. Born in Moscow in 1924, Shalamov studied at the Higher State Institute of Cinematography, and worked for many of the Soviet Union's best-read magazines and newspapers between 1951 and 1974. He has done freelance photographic work since his arrival in the United States, and lives in New York with his wife and son.

EMMANUEL ANTSIS, a filmmaker from Kiev, immigrated to the United States in 1979. Born in 1937, Antsis made numerous films for the Kiev Popular Science Film Studio, many of which won prizes at Soviet and international film festivals. His photographs were published in numerous Soviet magazines. Antsis, a bachelor, now lives in New York.

TANIA HULL was born in a small Russian town 150 miles from Moscow six years before the Bolshevik Revolution of 1917. Her father, an engineer, decided to flee Russia, taking his wife and six children to the Russian colony in Harbin, Manchuria. In 1935 the family moved again, to America, where Mrs. Hull adopted a new nationality and began a new life. After raising two children, Mrs. Hull became an avid amateur photographer, winning several prizes for her work. In 1977, forty years after she left, Mrs. Hull returned to Russia for a visit, taking along her cameras. Her photographs in this book were taken during that visit. Mrs. Hull lives with her husband of forty-one years in Columbia, Maryland.

VLADIMIR SICHOV, trained as a radio engineer and a former officer of the Soviet army, was born in 1945. Sichov grew up in a village on the coast of the Black Sea, and moved to Moscow only after his discharge from the army in 1971. He took photographs all over Russia between 1967 and 1979, when he emigrated from the USSR.

ALFRED TULCHINSKY received his first camera as a boy of twelve in his native Kharkov, and has been taking pictures ever since. Born in 1937, Tulchinsky studied and practiced architecture, then worked in television and journalism. From 1967 to 1971 he worked for the northernmost television station in the world, located in the Soviet city of Norilsk, just below the Arctic Circle. Tulchinsky's photographs appeared in many Soviet journals and exhibitions. He emigrated in 1978 and now lives in New York.

KALMAN KASPIEV, born in 1939, got his first experience as a photojournalist in Baku, the capital of Soviet Azerbaijan. He worked there for Tass, then moved to Moscow as a staff photographer for a popular picture magazine. Kaspiev's photographs have appeared in numerous Soviet and international exhibitions, and have been awarded many prizes. Kaspiev emigrated from the USSR in 1977 and now lives in New York.

LEV NISNEVICH began his career as a lighting technician at a Moscow film studio. After holding a variety of jobs as a journalist and photographer, he became a staff photographer for *Literary Gazette*, a popular weekly paper published in Moscow. In 1975 Nisnevich and his wife immigrated to the West. They now live in New York City.

IGOR PALMIN is a freelance photographer living in Moscow. His photographs of "unofficial" Soviet artists were shown at the Venice Biennale.

BARBARA GLUCK is a professional photographer now living in Santa Fe, New Mexico. Her work has appeared in the *New York Times*, *Newsweek*, the *Washington Post*, *Quest*, and many other journals, and in museum shows as well. Ms. Gluck took her cameras to the Soviet Union as a tourist.

ROGER SANDLER is a freelance photographer based in Los Angeles, whose pictures have been published by *Time, People, New West, Rolling Stone,* and many other journals. His pictures from the Soviet Union were taken on a tourist visit.

JEREMY STONE, the executive director of the Federation of American Scientists, is an avid amateur photographer and frequent visitor to the Soviet Union.

CHRISTOPHER OGDEN, now the White House correspondent of *Time* magazine, was based in Moscow in the early 1970s, where he took thousands of photographs.

GORDON JOSELOFF is serving his second tour of duty in the Soviet Union, this time as Moscow correspondent of CBS News.

ROBERT G. KAISER is the author of the text in this book.

KEVIN KLOSE is the Moscow correspondent of the *Washington Post.*

VLADIMIR GRIGOROVITCH is an artist who emigrated from the Soviet Union in 1972.

JOHN SHAW, an Australian now living in Canberra, was the Moscow correspondent of *Time* magazine.

STEVEN HOLMES was an American exchange student in Leningrad.

VITALI KOMAR and ALEXANDER MELAMID are Russian artists now living in New York who have collected thousands of photos of the Soviet Union.

The Death Penalty

Identifying Propaganda Techniques

The Death Penalty

Identifying Propaganda Techniques

Curriculum Consultant: JoAnne Buggey, Ph.D.
College of Education, University of Minnesota

By Carol O'Sullivan

Greenhaven Press, Inc.
Post Office Box 289009
San Diego, CA 92128-9009

Titles in the opposing viewpoints juniors series:

Smoking	Death Penalty
Gun Control	Drugs and Sports
Animal Rights	Toxic Wastes
AIDS	Patriotism
Alcohol	Working Mothers
Immigration	Terrorism

Cover photo: Wide World Photos

Library of Congress Cataloging-in-Publication Data

O'Sullivan, Carol, 1945–
    The death penalty : identifying propaganda techniques / by Carol
O'Sullivan.
       p.   cm. — (Opposing viewpoints juniors)
    ISBN 0-89908-494-X :
    1. Capital punishment—Juvenile literature.   [2. Critical thinking—
Juvenile literature.   3. Propaganda—Juvenile literature.
I. Title. II. Series.
HV8694.07 1989
364.6′6—dc20   89-11033
                                            CIP
                                            AC

CONTENTS

THE PURPOSE OF THIS BOOK

An Introduction to Opposing Viewpoints

When people disagree, it is hard to figure out who is right. You may decide one person is right just because the person is your friend or relative. But this is not a very good reason to agree or disagree with someone. It is better if you try to understand why these people disagree. On what main points do they differ? Read or listen to each person's argument carefully. Separate the facts and opinions that each person presents. Finally, decide which argument best matches what you think. This process, examining an argument without emotion, is part of what critical thinking is all about.

This is not easy. Many things make it hard to understand and form opinions. People's values, ages, and experiences all influence the way they think. This is why learning to read and think critically is an invaluable skill. Opposing Viewpoints Juniors books will help you learn and practice skills to improve your ability to read critically. By reading opposing views on an issue, you will become familiar with methods people use to attempt to convince you that their point of view is right. And you will learn to separate the authors' opinions from the facts they present.

Each Opposing Viewpoints Juniors book focuses on one critical thinking skill that will help you judge the views presented. Some of these skills are telling fact from opinion, recognizing propaganda techniques, and locating and analyzing the main idea. These skills will allow you to examine opposing viewpoints more easily.

Each viewpoint in this book is paraphrased from the original to make it easier to read. The viewpoints are placed in a running debate and are always placed with the pro view first.

What Are Propaganda Techniques?

Propaganda is information presented in an attempt to influence people. In this Opposing Viewpoints Juniors book, you will be asked to identify and study several common propaganda techniques. Some of these techniques appeal to your ability to think logically, while others appeal to your emotions. As an example, a car saleswoman who is telling you about a small economy car may say, "This car gets much better gas mileage than any car in its class." The saleswoman's argument for buying the car is based on her belief that you will make your car-buying decision logically. You will compare practical considerations such as mileage and initial cost. Another example is a car salesman who is telling you about a snazzy Maserati: "This car is the best-looking, fastest car ever made." His argument for buying the Maserati is based on his belief that you are considering such a car not for its practical qualities but because it excites you and is a status symbol.

In the examples above, the objective of both salespeople is to encourage you to buy a car. Both try to get you to focus on the most appealing quality of their cars—economy in the first example, flashiness in the second. Both ignore the disadvantages of their cars. In both cases, making a wise buying decision would mean getting more information. Since the car salespeople's objective is to get you to buy *their* car, you would need more objective sources, such as *Consumer Reports* magazine, to find out more facts.

DISTRACTING THE READER

All propaganda techniques, like those used by the car salespeople, distract the listener or reader from the complete picture. People who use propaganda techniques encourage you to look only at the factors that are important to accepting their argument as true.

Authors and speakers often use misleading propaganda techniques instead of offering legitimate proof for their arguments. The propaganda will be offered as a reason to believe the argument, but in reality will be weak, distracting, or irrelevant reasons. This Opposing Viewpoints Juniors book will focus on telling the difference between legitimate reasons to believe a particular argument and propaganda techniques that are used to mislead or distract you.

It is important to learn to recognize these techniques, especially when reading and evaluating differing opinions. This is because people who feel strongly about an issue use many of these techniques when attempting to persuade others to agree with their opinion. Some of these persuasive techniques may be relevant to your decision to agree, but others will not be. It is important to sift through the information, weeding the proof from the false reasoning.

While there are many types of propaganda techniques, this book will focus on three of them. These are *testimonial, bandwagon,* and *scare tactics.* Examples of these techniques are given below:

Testimonial—quoting or paraphrasing a celebrity or person in authority to support one's own argument. Often, the person being quoted is not qualified to express an opinion on the subject. For example, movie stars are often used to recommend a product they may know nothing about.

Sometimes, an actor or actress is dressed to look like an authority on the subject. For example, an actor will be dressed in a doctor's coat to recommend a pain medication in a TV commercial. The producers of the commercial believe you will assume the actor in a white coat is a doctor. They hope you will buy the pain medication because you trust doctors' opinions. But the truth is that the actor is not a doctor, has no knowledge of medicine, and is in no position to express an opinion. The commercial is deceptive—it asks you to accept the advice of someone who is not in a position to express an informed opinion.

But not all testimonials are used deceptively. Quoting a person who is truly an authority is a good way to support an argument. For instance, quoting a famous comedian like Richard Pryor about how drugs almost ruined his life would be an example of using a testimonial properly. He is in a position to give advice based on his personal experience. Also, quoting a dentist about how to prevent tooth decay is an example of a legitimate, or genuine, testimonial.

Bandwagon—suggesting that everybody else, or most people, or everybody in a certain group believes or acts a certain way, and therefore you should too. Bandwagon is a form of peer pressure that plays on a person's desire to be liked and respected. An example is, "Most people in our neighborhood have signed this petition to have a movie theater built. You should sign it, too."

Bandwagon arguments appeal to your sense of being part of the group, of being accepted. The purpose is to persuade you to do something just because everyone else is doing it. In the above example, the speaker tries to get you to sign a petition just because everyone else has signed it. But this is never a good reason to do something or believe something. You should consider all the evidence in a logical way and then decide for yourself. Whatever you decide, it should be your own opinion. It should not be based solely on what everyone else thinks is right.

Scare tactic—the threat that if you do not do or believe this, something terrible will happen. People using this technique will write or say alarming words and phrases to persuade you to believe their arguments. For example:

> Outer space has become our newest dumping ground. If we do not stop leaving pieces of rockets and other space junk in outer space, the sun will not be able to shine through our atmosphere. Without sunlight, we would die.

This is a deceptive argument. Considering the vastness of outer space and the power of the sun, it is unlikely that space debris could keep the sun from shining onto the earth. And no evidence is offered that this would be the case.

Authors who use scare tactics will often make up or exaggerate the frightening aspects of an issue. They want you to make a decision about the issue based on fear rather than on sound reasoning.

When reading differing arguments, then, there is a lot to think about. Are the authors giving sound reasons for their points of view? Or do they distort the importance of their arguments with propaganda techniques?

We asked two students to give their opinions on the death penalty issue. Look for examples of testimonial, bandwagon, and scare tactics in their arguments.

I think the death penalty is good.

I think the death penalty is the best punishment for murderers. My grandmother told me the Bible says "an eye for an eye, a tooth for a tooth." She says this means God thinks it's right to kill a person who has killed someone else.

I think the death penalty keeps people from killing other people. People would be afraid to kill someone because they would not want to be put to death.

There's another reason to kill murderers. By killing them, we make sure that they cannot murder anyone else. Sometimes murderers don't spend very much time in jail. Sometimes they even get to go home on weekends. The streets are probably full of murderers. Maybe they're looking for someone else to kill.

I think the death penalty is bad.

It's impossible to be sure someone is guilty of committing a crime. My friend Brian has an uncle who was blamed for killing someone. He almost had to go to the electric chair. Luckily, someone else confessed to the murder before Brian's uncle died. But if that person hadn't confessed, Brian's uncle would be dead today.

My dad says there's another reason for not letting the government kill people. He says the government already has too much power. Dad says soon the government will start telling us where we can live, what jobs we can do, and what books we can read.

Most other countries have stopped using the death penalty. These countries have lots of smart people who have thought about what's right and what's wrong. I think the United States should follow these countries and stop killing people.

Chip and Naomi have very different opinions about the death penalty. Both of them use propaganda techniques in their arguments:

Chip:

TESTIMONIAL

My grandmother told me the Bible says "an eye for an eye, a tooth for a tooth." She says this means God thinks it's right to kill a person who has killed someone else.

SCARE TACTIC

The streets are probably full of murderers.

Naomi:

TESTIMONIAL

My dad says there is another reason for not letting the government kill people. He says the government already has too much power.

BANDWAGON

Most other countries have stopped using the death penalty. . . . I think the United States should follow these countries and stop killing people.

In this sample, Chip and Naomi use some propaganda techniques when presenting their opinions. Both Chip and Naomi think they are right about the death penalty. What would you conclude about the death penalty from this sample? Why? As you continue to read through the viewpoints in this book, try keeping a tally like the one above to compare the authors' arguments.

CHAPTER 1

PREFACE: Should the Death Penalty Be Abolished?

A hotly-debated issue in our society is whether a person who commits a brutal crime, such as murder, should be punished by death.

The death penalty, also called "capital punishment," is not new to the United States. During most of the seventeenth and eighteenth centuries, the American colonies were under British rule. At that time, 200 different crimes were punishable by death. Among these crimes were stealing a loaf of bread and insulting the Crown.

The laws have softened since the eighteenth century. Criminals are no longer executed for petty crimes. But many people argue that executing criminals for any crime is wrong. These people claim that the death penalty should be abolished, or ended, because it is not only immoral but also illegal. They say it violates the Eighth Amendment to the Constitution. This amendment forbids cruel and unusual punishments. It is stated as follows:

> Excessive bail shall not be required, nor excessive fines imposed, nor cruel and unusual punishments inflicted.

On the other side are people who favor the death penalty. These people claim that executing criminals is neither cruel nor unusual as long as the criminals do not suffer physical pain. Those who favor the death penalty further argue that it does no good to put murderers in jail. Society is not protected from them because they get released from jail in a few years. Then they are back on the streets committing more crimes.

The death penalty is an emotional issue. Arguments for and against it use many propaganda techniques. In the next two viewpoints, look for examples of testimonial, scare tactics, and bandwagon.

The death penalty should be abolished

Editor's Note: This viewpoint is paraphrased from an article written by a member of Amnesty International. Amnesty International is a human rights organization that opposes the death penalty. In this viewpoint, the author tells why the death penalty should be ended.

More and more prisoners in the United States are being executed for their crimes. At least sixty-six people have been executed since 1976. Nearly two thousand more are on death row. They are waiting to be electrocuted, gassed, poisoned, hanged, or shot.

It is true that most of the criminals on death row have been convicted of brutal crimes. But killing a person is not proper punishment for any crime. It is a violation of the basic right to life. And, it is illegal. The Constitution of the United States forbids cruel and unusual punishment. Robbing a person of his or her life is certainly cruel and unusual.

Besides ending their lives, executions also cause prisoners physical pain. This, too, is cruel and unusual. Some examples of this suffering are:

> In a 1983 electrocution in Alabama, three charges of nineteen hundred volts of electricity and fourteen minutes were needed to kill the prisoner. After the second charge, smoke and flames burst from his head and left leg.

> In a 1983 execution by poisonous gas in Mississippi, the prisoner shook violently for eight minutes. He kept hitting his head on a pole behind him before he died.

"Fetch me the law for the rich, will you?"

© Punch/Rothco

This cruelty is reason enough to put an end to the death penalty. But there is another reason. The death penalty is not handed out fairly. The evidence suggests that the use of the death penalty has become a horrifying "lottery." Luck and the circumstances of a person's life often determine whether he or she will live or die.

For example, it is not fair that poor people are executed a lot more often than rich people. In fact, a former governor of Ohio said, "I have found that men on death row had one thing in common: they were penniless . . . the fact that they had no money was a principal factor in their being condemned to death." This belief is also expressed by a former warden of San Quentin prison in California. He said that the death penalty is "a privilege of the poor."

Also, it is not fair that people with mental illness are often not even aware that they have done anything wrong. Yet, many are executed right along with people who know right from wrong.

Finally, it is not fair that when two people commit a crime, sometimes only one person is executed for it. In one case, a prisoner was executed for murder even though his partner committed the crime. The prisoner was not even in the room when the killing happened. But the court said the prisoner was guilty because he should have known his partner was capable of killing. In another case, a killer's partner was executed for a murder while the killer himself was given only a life sentence.

Perhaps the most important reason for ending the death penalty is that innocent people are sometimes executed. Records show that at least twenty-three people in the United States have been killed for crimes they did not commit.

Executions in the United States are increasing. However, in the rest of the civilized world, they are decreasing. Many other countries are completely doing away with the death penalty. France ended the death penalty in 1981. Britain ended it in 1969. In fact, at least one country a year has put an end to the death penalty since 1975. It is time the United States did the same.

The author says the death penalty is handed out unfairly. Does he offer proof that this is the case? Is this a scare tactic?

Does the governor's testimonial persuade you to agree with the author that the death penalty should be abolished? Why or why not?

Do you think a prison warden knows which prisoners are most often executed? Is he in a position to give an informed opinion on the death penalty? Why or why not?

The author tells us that many other countries are getting rid of the death penalty and that the United States should too. Which propaganda technique is he using?

Is the death penalty handed out unfairly?

The author gives four reasons for why the death penalty is handed out unfairly. Can you name these four reasons? Which of these four reasons is the most convincing? Why?

The death penalty should not be abolished

Editor's Note: This viewpoint is paraphrased from an article that appeared in *Lincoln Review* journal. In it, the author explains why the death penalty is needed in America and why arguments against the death penalty are weak.

The author says murder has become an epidemic in our society. Is he using a scare tactic? Why or why not?

The death penalty is being debated in the United States. Because many people oppose the death penalty, few murderers have been executed. The result is that murder has become an epidemic in our society.

More people are murdered in the U.S. than have been killed in some war zones. For example, during the German bombardment of London in the years 1940–1945, there were 21.7 deaths per 100,000 people. In Detroit, for the years 1973–1978, there were 42.4 deaths per 100,000 people from murder.

People who oppose the death penalty cite many reasons for wanting to end this form of punishment. They argue that the death penalty violates the Eighth Amendment to the Constitution. This amendment forbids using cruel or unusual methods to punish criminals.

But people who use the Eighth Amendment argument forget an important fact. This amendment was made part of the Constitution in 1791. At that time, governments throughout the world did punish criminals cruelly and unusually.

One of these methods of punishment was burning the victim. Another method was impaling—throwing the victim on a sharp stake. A third method was pressing—piling rocks on top of the victim until he or she could not breathe. But today, Americans do not use cruel forms of punishment. Therefore, modern executions in the United States do not violate the Eighth Amendment.

Opponents of the death penalty have another reason for wanting to end it. They say killing a human being for any reason is immoral. These people argue that executing murderers is against the religious tradition of America.

But C. S. Lewis, a Christian writer, disagrees. He says that the "human feeling that bad men ought to suffer" does not go against our religious beliefs. And St. Paul wrote that governments are appointed by God to carry out His punishment. Therefore, the government is doing God's will by executing murderers. Finally, Jesus Christ said, "All who take the sword will perish by the sword." This can be interpreted to mean Jesus thought that murderers deserve to die.

People who think the death penalty is immoral say that putting a murderer in prison for life is punishment enough. But there is a problem with this punishment. Most murderers sentenced to life in prison are released. In New York, prisoners serving life sentences can be released in just nineteen months.

Robert Johnson, assistant professor of justice at American University's School of Justice, said that most criminals are no longer given true life sentences. He said that most prisoners convicted of murder serve only seven to fourteen years in jail.

People who oppose the death penalty have one more reason for wanting to end it. They say that fear of the death penalty does not stop murderers from killing their victims. This may be true in some cases. But most people, including murderers, are afraid to die. Ernest van den Haag, a professor at Fordham University, wrote, "Common sense . . . tells us that the death penalty will deter murder, if anything can. People fear nothing more than death."

The author quotes religious authorities. Do you think these testimonials prove that these people approved of the death penalty? Why or why not?

Which propaganda technique is the author using in this paragraph?

Ernest van den Haag is a Distinguished Scholar at The Heritage Foundation and a law professor at Fordham University. He has also authored many books and articles on the death penalty. He is considered an authority on the death penalty. Does his testimonial support the author's argument that the death penalty is necessary?

Dick Locher. Reprinted by permission: Tribune Media Services.

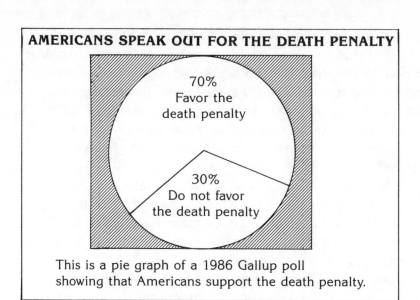

AMERICANS SPEAK OUT FOR THE DEATH PENALTY

70%
Favor the
death penalty

30%
Do not favor
the death penalty

This is a pie graph of a 1986 Gallup poll
showing that Americans support the death penalty.

SOURCE: 1986 Gallup poll

The author says the majority of Americans believe murderers deserve to die. He is implying that you should believe this too. Which propaganda technique is he using?

Does Senator McClellan's testimonial persuade you to agree with the author's argument that the death penalty is necessary? Why or why not?

Despite these arguments against the death penalty, the overwhelming majority of Americans believe murderers deserve to die for their crimes. Recent polls indicate that 72 percent of Americans are in favor of the death penalty. In fact, a majority of all groups, including blacks and whites, men and women, support the death penalty.

Some Americans have even said that there is no other just punishment for murder than the death penalty. In a debate on the subject, the late Democratic Senator John McClellan, referring to some particularly brutal murders, asked: "What other punishment is 'just' for a man . . . who would stab, strangle, and mutilate eight student nurses? What other punishment is 'just' for a band of social misfits who would invade the homes of people they had never even met and stab and hack to death a pregnant woman and her guests?"

It is time we reject the idea that murderers should not be executed. Most of these cruel killers cannot change their behavior. It is our duty to remove them from society so they can never kill again. And only the death penalty can ensure that they are removed.

Edward Koch, mayor of New York City, agrees. He said that we must apply the death penalty in certain cases if we are ever to have a civilized society where people do not kill each other.

Which propaganda technique is the author using here?

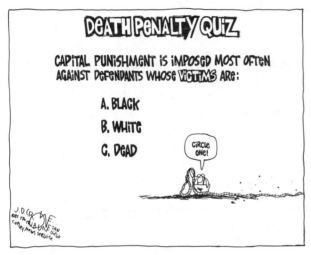

J. D. Crowe. Reprinted with permission.

Is the death penalty necessary?

The author first discusses his opponents' arguments against the death penalty and then tells why he thinks his opponents' arguments are weak. Find an example of this in the text.

What reasons does the author give for why we need to use the death penalty on murderers?

Identifying Propaganda Techniques

After reading the two viewpoints on whether the death penalty should be abolished, make a chart similar to the one made for Chip and Naomi on page 10. List one example of each propaganda technique for each author's viewpoint. A chart is started for you below:

Amnesty International:

TESTIMONIAL

A former warden of San Quentin Prison in California said that the death penalty is "a privilege of the poor."

Lincoln Review:

SCARE TACTIC

Murder has become an epidemic in our society.

After completing your chart, answer the following questions. Which article used the most propaganda techniques? Which article was the most convincing? Why? Which one did you personally agree with?

CHAPTER

PREFACE: **Should the Death Penalty Be Used for Some Crimes?**

In the late 1800s, juries were required to impose the death penalty for various crimes including murders in which the killer meant to kill the victim. In the early 1900s, the laws changed. Jurors were allowed to consider the circumstances of the murder and then decide whether to sentence a murderer to death or to life in prison.

But many people wanted the death penalty ended altogether. They insisted that all executions were immoral and illegal. As a result, in 1967 the federal courts suspended all death sentences until the Supreme Court could decide whether the death penalty was legal.

In 1976, the Supreme Court decided that the death penalty was legal, but that it was at times handed out unfairly. This court established new rules and guidelines to be followed in murder cases to ensure that the death penalty is handed out fairly.

But many people feel that these new guidelines and regulations do not make the death penalty moral. They believe that killing another human being is always wrong. These people oppose the death penalty for all criminal cases.

On the other side are people who agree that some murderers do not deserve the death penalty. But these people disagree that the death penalty should never be used. They believe it is necessary to execute criminals who have committed particularly bad crimes. They argue that these criminals will not change their behavior and will always be a threat to society.

The next two viewpoints debate whether the death penalty should be required in some cases.

The death penalty is necessary for some crimes

Editor's Note: This viewpoint is paraphrased from an article by Frank B. Roome, a convicted murderer serving a sentence at the Kansas Correctional Institution in Lansing. In this viewpoint, Mr. Roome explains why he believes some criminals should be executed.

I am a convicted murderer. I am serving a sentence at the Kansas Correctional Institution. As a prisoner, I have lost many rights. But I still have the right to express my opinion. And I believe that the death penalty is the only appropriate punishment for certain crimes.

One of these crimes is murder committed for money. This includes murders committed during robberies and kidnappings. It also includes murders for hire.

Most murders are sad acts of anger. They involve people killing their friends and family during arguments. These murderers deserve to be treated with sympathy. But there are other killers who deserve no sympathy. These are the men and women who kill for money, without the slightest regard for human life. I know such people exist. I have lived among them.

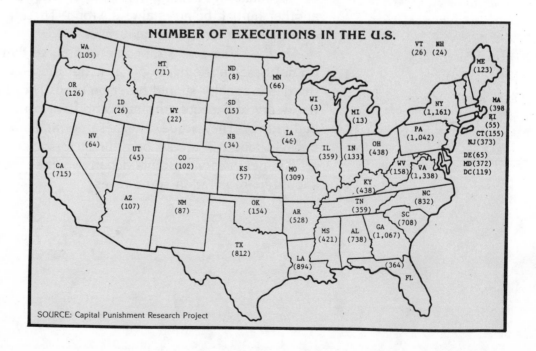

NUMBER OF EXECUTIONS IN THE U.S.

WA (105)
OR (126)
MT (71)
ND (8)
MN (66)
VT (26)
NH (24)
ME (123)
ID (26)
WY (22)
SD (15)
WI (3)
NY (1,161)
MA (398)
RI (55)
NV (64)
UT (45)
CO (102)
NB (34)
IA (46)
MI (13)
PA (1,042)
CT (155)
NJ (373)
CA (715)
KS (57)
MO (309)
IL (359)
IN (133)
OH (438)
WV (158)
VA (1,338)
DE (65)
MD (372)
DC (119)
AZ (107)
NM (87)
OK (154)
AR (528)
KY (438)
TN (359)
NC (832)
SC (708)
MS (421)
AL (738)
GA (1,067)
TX (812)
LA (894)
FL (364)

SOURCE: Capital Punishment Research Project

I also support the death penalty for a prisoner who kills another person while in prison. These murderers are usually serving life sentences. They have nothing to lose by killing someone. Only the threat of the death penalty might stop them from killing fellow prisoners and guards.

Finally, I support the death penalty for murderers who commit more than one murder in a short period of time. For these people, murder has become a horrible hobby. I believe all these criminals deserve the death penalty for their crimes. Many other intelligent, thoughtful people agree with me. The Greek philosophers Plato and Aristotle supported the death penalty. So did St. Thomas Aquinas, Thomas More, the English statesman, and John Locke, the English philosopher.

The death penalty is fair punishment for some criminals. And it also saves the government money. It costs ten thousand dollars a year to keep a prisoner in jail until he dies. This amounts to five hundred thousand dollars or more for many prisoners. This is money taken from America's schools, hospitals, and the elderly.

A final reason for applying the death penalty is that it is actually more humane than keeping a person in prison for life. Sentencing a person to prison for life forces him or her to live without hope. He or she must endure unending years in an environment fit only for animals. A punishment that reduces a person to something less than human cannot be just.

I realize that most people do not like to think about the death penalty. It is unpleasant. But most modern societies do rob people of their lives. Our young die in far-off lands in wars. Their only "crime" is being too young to get out of going to war. We execute these young people by sending them to war. Why, then, don't we want to execute criminals?

Do you agree that people who commit more than one murder have chosen murder as a hobby? Is the author using a scare tactic?

The author is implying that intelligent, thoughtful people support the death penalty, and that you should too if you want to be considered intelligent and thoughtful. Which propaganda technique is the author using?

The author implies that if we keep prisoners in jail, we will not have enough money for our schools, hospitals, and elderly. Is he using a scare tactic? Why or why not?

Which crimes are punishable by death?

Name the three crimes Mr. Roome thinks deserve the death penalty. Do you agree? Do you think there are any crimes that deserve the death penalty? What are these crimes?

Editor's Note: This viewpoint is paraphrased from an article by Mary Meehan, a writer. In this viewpoint, Ms. Meehan discusses why she believes the death penalty should never be used. Some of the testimonials will be discussed in the focus box at the end of the reading.

Which propaganda technique is the author using in this paragraph?

Charles Peguy was a French poet and writer who wrote about people's rights. Does his testimonial persuade you to agree with the author that criminals should never be executed? Why or why not?

Criminals should never be given the death penalty for their crimes. There are many good reasons to oppose this form of punishment.

One of the most important reasons is that people have been executed for crimes they did not commit. Many of these people were found innocent after someone else admitted committing the crime.

Watt Espy, a researcher who has studied American executions, says he believes that ten innocent men were executed in Alabama alone. Mr. Espy cites names, dates, and other specifics of the cases. He adds that there are similar cases in almost every state.

What do we say after we have executed an innocent person? Do we write "I'm sorry" on his tombstone? What do we say to his widow and children?

The wrongful taking of a life by a country's government is a disgrace to the people of that country. We might consider Charles Peguy's words about the French case in which Captain Alfred Dreyfus was wrongly convicted of treason. Peguy said, "a single legal crime, a single dishonorable act will bring about the loss of one's honor, the dishonor of a whole people."

RACIAL BIAS?
The death row population continues to increase. More blacks are executed.

Inmates on Death Row

White
Black
Hispanic

1977   79   81   83   85   87

1,000
750
500
250
0

SOURCE: NAACP

Another reason for opposing the death penalty is that racial discrimination, or prejudice, is often used in deciding who dies and who does not. In the U.S., black people are given the death penalty more often than others. Of the 1,058 prisoners on death row in 1982, 42 percent were black. Only 12 percent of the U.S. population is black.

Walter Berns is a scholar who favors executing certain criminals. Yet he admits that judges and juries have used racial discrimination in handing out the death penalty. He told the Senate Judiciary Committee that the death penalty has been handed out to people in an unfair way in the United States.

Besides being unfair to blacks, the death penalty is also immoral. Many religions are against it. Former Iowa Senator Harold Hughes says the death penalty goes against the teaching of the Bible. He said, "'Thou shalt not kill' is the shortest of the Ten Commandments. . . . It is as clear . . . as the powerful thrust of chain lightning out of a dark summer sky." St. John, too, believed that no one has the right to kill another person. He wrote, "He that is without sin among you, let him cast the first stone."

The death penalty is immoral for another reason. It forces doctors to kill people. Doctors have to give the condemned prisoners shots of poison. This is wrong. Doctors are supposed to save people. The American Medical Association agrees. In 1980, the AMA said that doctors should not take part in an execution.

Many people oppose the death penalty. Even those people who are not "soft on crime" are against criminal execution. They do not think people have the right to play God. And they do not believe the government encourages respect for life when it kills people.

Albert Camus was a French writer and philosopher who died in 1960. He opposed the death penalty. Camus said, "We know enough to say that some crimes require severe punishment. We do not know enough to say when anyone should die." Camus was right.

Walter Berns is a scholar and writer who is considered an authority on the death penalty. Does his testimonial support the author's argument that the death penalty should never be applied?

Carol*Simpson/Rothco

The author says that many people oppose the death penalty. Is this a good reason for you to oppose it? Why or why not?

Is the death penalty wrong?

Ms. Meehan uses many testimonials in this viewpoint. Can you point out two of them in addition to the ones already mentioned? Analyze these two testimonials. Are either of them used deceptively? Why or why not?

2

Understanding Editorial Cartoons

Throughout this book you will see cartoons that illustrate the ideas in the viewpoints. Editorial cartoons are an effective and usually humorous way of presenting an opinion on an issue. Cartoonists, like writers, can use ways of persuading you that include propaganda techniques. While many cartoons are easy to understand, others, like the one below, require more thought.

Look at the two frames of the cartoon below. The cartoonist has drawn a frightening creature to represent people's urge to kill. What has been added to the second frame that does not appear in the first? Do you think the cartoonist approves or disapproves of the death penalty? Why? Does the cartoon persuade you to share the cartoonist's view on the death penalty? Why or why not?

'BAD'

'GOOD'

© Miller/Rothco

3

PREFACE: Does the Death Penalty Cause Murder?

A study was undertaken in the early 1980s to determine the effects of the death penalty on murder. The study found that between the years 1957 and 1965, when the death penalty was being used to punish murderers, 78,600 murders were committed in the U.S., and 337 people were executed. Between 1967 and 1976, when the Supreme Court suspended all executions, 159,600 murders were committed, and no people were executed.

People who favor the death penalty say that these statistics prove that the death penalty prevents murder. They point out that when people are executed for murder, the murder rate throughout the country decreases. On the other hand, when fewer people are executed for murder, the murder rate increases.

Other people argue that the death penalty increases murder. They acknowledge that when the number of executions goes up, the number of murders throughout the country goes down. But these people argue that important evidence is ignored. This evidence is that when an execution occurs in a certain city, the murder rate in that city goes up. This, they say, is proof that the death penalty encourages citizens to use violence as a solution to problems. The citizens believe that if the government can kill someone, it must be all right.

The next two viewpoints debate these issues. Pay close attention to the propaganda techniques the authors use.

Editor's Note: This viewpoint is paraphrased from an article by Louis Joylon West, chairman of the department of psychiatry and biobehavioral sciences at the University of California, Los Angeles Medical Center. In this viewpoint, Dr. West argues that the death penalty causes people to commit murder and that it should be ended.

Is the author using a propaganda technique in this paragraph? If so, which one?

The author says citizens accept killing as a solution to problems. Is he using a propaganda technique? If so, which one?

The death penalty should be abolished totally and permanently. There are many reasons why this is true. Perhaps the most difficult to understand is that the death penalty causes murder. The majority of scholars, governors, wardens, crime experts, jurists, and social scientists share this opinion.

When prisoners are executed, citizens accept killing as a solution to problems. This has been proved. Facts show that when an execution takes place, the murder rate goes up in that city. People think that if the government can kill someone, so can they.

But there is an even more specific way in which the death penalty causes murder. Some people who commit murder are actually trying to commit suicide. They believe if they kill someone they themselves will die because the government will execute them as punishment for their crime.

One example of this is a murderer named James French. French killed a driver who had stopped to pick him up while he was hitchhiking in Oklahoma. French asked to be executed for his crime. But he received a life sentence instead. French was outraged. After three years in prison, he strangled his cell mate. He admitted he did it just so he could be executed. In 1966, he got his wish. He was the only man executed during that year.

If the death penalty did not exist, the men French murdered would probably still be alive. It is likely that more people will be killed by murderers seeking their own deaths.

Is this a scare tactic? Why or why not?

There are other examples of how the death penalty causes violence. One day a farmer walked into a roadside cafe in Texas. He aimed a shotgun at a man sitting at the lunch counter and killed him. He did not even know the man. When asked why he did it, he replied, "I was just tired of living."

In some cases, people who seek their own deaths even confess to a murder they did not commit. One such man was Joseph Shay. In 1966, Shay admitted that he had falsely confessed to an unsolved murder. He said he did it "because I wanted to die."

It is a fact that violent crime is part of our society. We are filled with sympathy for victims and their families. But the prisoner convicted of a violent crime is in prison. Society is safe from him. There is no reason to execute him.

There has been a trend toward ending the death penalty in countries in the Western world. These countries have fewer violent crimes than the United States. Most of these countries have many other laws that show mercy for their citizens.

Other countries are ending the death penalty. Is this a good enough reason for the United States to end it? Which propaganda technique is the author using?

Albert Camus, the French writer, opposed the death penalty. Camus believed the death penalty causes violence in societies. He said we have to end the death penalty if we ever hope to end war.

Which propaganda technique is the author using in this paragraph?

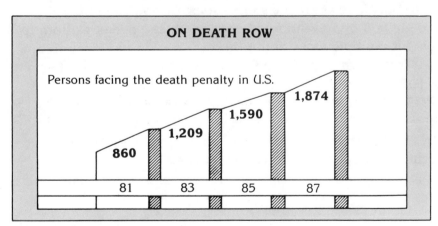

ON DEATH ROW

Persons facing the death penalty in U.S.

1,874
1,590
1,209
860

81   83   85   87

SOURCE: US Dept. of Justice. NAACP Legal Defense and Educational Fund

Does the death penalty cause murder?

Mr. West cites two reasons for why the death penalty causes people to commit murder. What are these two reasons?

Editor's Note: This viewpoint is paraphrased from an article by Karl Spence. When he wrote this article, Mr. Spence was a student at Texas A & M University. Mr. Spence cites studies that prove that when the death penalty is enforced, murder decreases.

Violent crime has become a normal occurrence in the United States. Mass murder is so common that multiple killings often do not even make the headlines. The verb "to mug" has entered our vocabulary. Slaughtering and robbing American citizens has become part of the American way of life.

What is so horrifying is that people do not seem to care if their fellow citizens become crime victims. Skid row drunks are tortured to death. Young women are raped and strangled. Whole families are murdered in their beds, while the rest of us go on about our business.

In the fall of 1976, an elderly couple in New York City was robbed and tortured two different times in their own apartment. They finally hanged themselves. They said they did not want "to live in fear anymore."

There is still no agreement as to what causes crime in America. But there are many suggestions for how to prevent it.

One method of preventing crime is to defend ourselves from it. We can put multiple locks on our homes. We can use electronic security systems at airports and banks. We can try to control who owns guns. But these tactics make us feel like we are in constant danger. They make us think we have to be suspicious of our neighbors. Soon, we will believe we cannot trust anyone. This feeling that we cannot trust anyone is perhaps the most evil consequence of our failure to control crime.

The only thing that will prevent crime is punishment. For violent crimes, the death penalty is the answer.

Does the author's evidence prove that slaughtering and robbing have become the American way of life? Is this a propaganda technique? If so, which one?

THE DEATH PENALTY AND ITS EFFECT ON MURDER

32%
Believe death penalty does not prevent murder

7% Have no opinion

61% Believe death penalty prevents murder

This pie graph shows how Americans voted in the 1986 Gallup poll on whether they believe the death penalty prevents murder.

SOURCE: 1986 Gallup Poll

Is the author using a propaganda technique? If so, which one?

Many American people oppose the death penalty. They hate the idea of execution as much as they hate crime. But the majority of Americans accept the death penalty as just punishment for some crimes. All Americans should support the death penalty.

People who oppose the death penalty say it does not prevent murder. But statistics prove that this is not true. A study of the relationship between the death penalty and murder shows that when more criminals are given the death penalty, fewer murders are committed. Likewise, when fewer criminals are executed, more murders are committed. For example, in 1957, there were 65 executions and 8,060 murders in the United States. In 1966, there was one execution and 10,920 murders, and in 1980, there were no executions and 23,040 murders.

Criminals do not want to die any more than anyone else. So, if they know they will receive the death penalty for killing someone, they probably will not do it.

A bloodbath is taking place in our country. In six months, more Americans are murdered than have died from the death penalty in this entire country. If we do not execute their murderers, these killings will continue. Until we begin to fight crime, every person who dies at a criminal's hands is the victim of our inaction. We must take responsibility for their deaths.

The late J. Edgar Hoover, former director of the F.B.I., agreed that we must take strong action against criminals. He said crime is a dangerous condition that will destroy our country if it is not ended soon.

Which propaganda technique is the author using in this paragraph?

Is the author using a propaganda technique in this paragraph? If so, which one?

Is this an example of a legitimate testimonial? Why or why not?

Are all testimonials the same?

Many of the testimonials you have read in these viewpoints are statements by people such as prison wardens and law professors who are somehow involved professionally with the criminal justice system. Other testimonials are by writers, poets, and philosophers who have no professional connection with the justice system, but who have spent much time thinking about and writing about solutions to social problems such as crime. Which group—the crime professionals or the writers and philosophers—do you think is in the best position to express informed opinions on the death penalty? Why?

Identifying Propaganda Techniques

This activity will allow you to practice identifying propaganda techniques. The statements below focus on the subject matter of this chapter—the effects of the death penalty on murder. Each statement is an example of bandwagon, scare tactic, or testimonial. Mark "B" next to any statement you believe is an example of bandwagon, "S" next to any statement you believe is a scare tactic, and "T" next to any statement you believe is a testimonial.

Answer

EXAMPLE: A warden at Garden State Prison said, "I have known people who have confessed to crimes they did not commit because they wanted to be executed."   T

1. Everyone in Mr. Lewis's first-grade class thinks the death penalty causes murder. You should agree with Mr. Lewis's class.   _____

2. Pope John Paul II had this to say about the death penalty, "It does not matter whether the fear of death would prevent murder, what matters is that killing people for any reason is immoral."   _____

3. If we let murderers back on the streets, chances are they will murder everyone in the U.S.   _____

4. J. Edgar Hoover, former director of the F.B.I., said that the death penalty prevents murder.   _____

5. Most intelligent people agree that killing a murderer is the only way to be sure he or she will not kill again. Anyone who disagrees with this is stupid.   _____

6. If we let the government keep killing people for crimes, someday it might start killing people for bad driving.   _____